instant manager
taking control of work and life

Cha...
management
institute
inspiring leaders

body
LANGUAGE

GEOFF RIBBENS & GREG WHITEAR

...nold

...LINE GROUP

The publisher has used its best endeavours to ensure that the URLs for external websites referred to in this book are correct and active at the time of going to press. However, the publisher and the authors have no responsibility for the websites and can make no guarantee that a site will remain live or that the content will remain relevant, decent or appropriate.

Orders: Please contact Bookpoint Ltd, 130 Milton Park, Abingdon, Oxon OX14 4SB. Telephone: (44) 01235 827720, Fax: (44) 01235 400454. Lines are open from 9.00 to 5.00, Monday to Saturday, with a 24-hour message answering service. You can also order through our website www.hoddereducation.co.uk.

British Library Cataloguing in Publication Data
A catalogue record for this title is available from the British Library.

ISBN-13: 978 0340 945 711

First published in UK 2007 by Hodder Education, 338 Euston Road, London NW1 3BH in association with the Chartered Management Institute.

Copyright © 2007 Geoff Ribbens and Greg Whitear

Typeset by Transet Limited, Coventry, England.
Printed in Great Britain for Hodder Education, a division of Hodder Headline, an Hachette Livre UK Company, 338 Euston Road, London NW1 3BH by Cox & Wyman Ltd, Reading, Berkshire.

Hodder Headline's policy is to use papers that are natural, renewable and recyclable products and made from wood grown in sustainable forests. The logging and manufacturing processes are expected to conform to the environmental regulations of the country of origin.

Impression number   10 9 8 7 6 5 4 3 2 1
Year   2012 2011 2010 2009 2008 2007

The Chartered
Management Institute

chartered

management

institute

inspiring leaders

The Chartered Management Institute is the only chartered professional body that is dedicated to management and leadership. We are committed to raising the performance of business by championing management.

We represent 71,000 individual managers and have 450 corporate members. Within the Institute there are also a number of distinct specialisms, including the Institute of Business Consulting and Women in Management Network.

We exist to help managers tackle the management challenges they face on a daily basis by raising the standard of management in the UK. We are here to help individuals become better managers and companies develop better managers.

We do this through a wide range of products and services, from practical management checklists to tailored training and qualifications. We produce research on the latest 'hot' management issues, provide a vast array of useful information through our online management information centre, as well as offering consultancy services and career information.

You can access these resources 'off the shelf' or we can provide solutions just for you. Our range of products and services is designed to ensure companies and managers develop their potential and excel. Whether you are at the start of your career or a proven performer in the boardroom, we have something for you.

We engage policy makers and opinion formers and, as the leading authority on management, we are regularly consulted on a range of management issues. Through our in-depth research and regular policy surveys of members, we have a deep understanding of the latest management trends.

For more information visit our website **www.managers.org.uk** or call us on **01536 207307**.

Chartered Manager

Transform the way you work

The Chartered Management Institute's Chartered Manager award is the ultimate accolade for practising professional managers. Designed to transform the way you think about your work and how you add value to your organisation, it is based on demonstrating measurable impact.

This unique award proves your ability to make a real difference in the workplace.

Chartered Manager focuses on the six vital business skills of:

- Leading people
- Managing change
- Meeting customer needs
- Managing information and knowledge
- Managing activities and resources
- Managing yourself

Transform your organisation

There is a clear and well-established link between good management and improved organisational performance. Recognising this, the Chartered Manager scheme requires individuals to demonstrate how they are applying their leadership and change management skills to make significant impact within their organisation.

Transform your career

Whatever career stage a manager is at Chartered Manager will set them apart. Chartered Manager has proven to be a stimulus to career progression, either via recognition by their current employer or through the motivation to move on to more challenging roles with new employers.

But don't take just our word for it ...

Chartered Manager has transformed the careers and organisations of managers in all sectors.

- *'Being a Chartered Manager was one of the main contributing factors which led to my recent promotion.'*
  Lloyd Ross, Programme Delivery Manager, British Nuclear Fuels

- *'I am quite sure that a part of the reason for my success in achieving my appointment was due to my Chartered Manager award which provided excellent independent evidence that I was a high quality manager.'*
  Donaree Marshall, Head of Programme Management Office, Water Service, Belfast

- *'The whole process has been very positive, giving me confidence in my strengths as a manager but also helping me to identify the areas of my skills that I want to develop. I am delighted and proud to have the accolade of Chartered Manager.'*
  Allen Hudson, School Support Services Manager, Dudley Metropolitan County Council

- *'As we are in a time of profound change, I believe that I have, as a result of my change management skills, been able to provide leadership to my staff. Indeed, I took over three teams and carefully built an integrated team, which is beginning to perform really well. I believe that the process I went through to gain Chartered Manager status assisted me in achieving this and consequently was of considerable benefit to my organisation.'*
  George Smart, SPO and D/Head of Resettlement, HM Prison Swaleside.

To find out more or to request further information please visit our website **www.managers.org.uk/cmgr** or call us on **01536 207429**.

Contents

CHAPTER 03

CHAPTER 04

CHAPTER 05

HOW CAN BODY LANGUAGE HELP ME IN INTERVIEWING, COUNSELLING AND FEEDBACK? 68

CHAPTER 06

HOW CAN BODY LANGUAGE HELP ME IN MEETINGS AND PRESENTATIONS? 83

CHAPTER 07

HOW CAN BODY LANGUAGE HELP ME IN SELLING? 103

CHAPTER 10

HOW CAN BODY LANGUAGE HELP ME WORK WITH PEOPLE FROM DIFFERENT CULTURES?

Preface

This book has been written to show the relevance of body language in the manager's day-to-day activities, such as running meetings, interviewing, giving presentations, selling, negotiating, working abroad, office life, security and control, as well as office politics.

Both authors are experienced management consultants and trainers and have related what they know about organisational behaviour and interpersonal skills to body language: an aspect of communication and influence which is largely taken for granted.

The book is a larger version, with additional chapters, of the Hodder Arnold book, *Body Language* by Geoff Ribbens and Richard Thompson, published in association with the Chartered Management Institute in 2000.

We would like to thank Greg's wife, Jacquie, for the many hours she has spent proofreading our writing and improving the text to make it more readable and understandable. Also thanks to Geoff's wife, Janice, for allowing him to work at the weekends to complete the book and for shielding him from the exigencies of grandchildren.

We would like to think Pat Weedon of Oxford Designers and Illustrators for preparing the excellent drawings that add clarity and meaning to our descriptions of body language.

Finally, we would like to thank Alison Frecknall, editor of the Instant Manager Series, for her support, patience and encouragement.

Geoff Ribbens
Greg Whitear

What is body language and why is it important in the work setting?

To some extent the term 'body language' is a misnomer, and so is the other, widely used academic term, 'non-verbal communications'. Both terms refer to the fact that when people communicate, the meanings, feelings, emotions and attitudes that are conveyed are often transmitted, not by the words that are used, but by a multitude of gestures, postures, facial expressions and eye movements, as well as the speed and intonation of the voice. Body language actually includes more than body movements and non-verbal communications; it also includes 'verbal' elements such as grunts and sighs.

What do we mean by body language?

In this book we will use the term 'body language' to include all methods of communication that do not reside in the words themselves. These are the postures, gestures, grunts, sighs, eye movements, speed of voice, tone of voice, pronunciation of words and so forth. It is the non-verbal elements of communication that supply the meaning, feeling, mood, intention and attitude of the supplier of the message and indeed the receiver of the message.

In nearly all books on body language it is suggested that in face-to-face communication about ten per cent of the communication is from the words that are used, 30 per cent is from the tone and speed of voice and the remaining 60 per cent is from the physical postures, gestures, and facial expressions etc.

We have not seen research evidence to support this often-quoted figure, but believe that it originates from Professor Albert Mehrabian's work in 1981, which he titled *Silent Messages*, and in which he quotes similar figures for 'verbal liking', 'vocal liking' and 'facial liking'. It must be very difficult to study meaning and feeling scientifically, whether conveyed by how we use words or by the body language that is exhibited. However, such a large percentage of the communication process attributed to non-verbal means is not actually surprising, especially if we consider what body language actually refers to:

- **Gestures** – the movements of the hands, head and body that add emphasis to a communication.
- **Expressions** – the arrangement of the face and eye movements that convey a great deal of the meaning of a communication.
- **Stances** – a set of gestures and expressions that make up typical body postures, such as aggression, assertiveness, fear, concern, relaxed, happy etc.

- **Distance** – the amount of space between those who are interacting.
- **Vocal** – the volume, tone, inflection, speed and pause elements of spoken communication.
- **Utterances** – the non-verbal sounds that convey meaning, such as grunts, sighs, growls, whistles etc.

The last two on the list above are not words themselves but convey a great deal to the meaning of communication. These elements are referred to as 'para-linguistic cues'.

It can be truly said that people 'dance' and 'sing' to the 'tune' of their 'thoughts'.

A note about the way we speak – our para-linguistic cues

As the old saying goes: 'It's not what you say, it's the way that you say it.'

In many cases you can totally change the meaning of a word by how you say it. Let us take a simple word like 'Yes'.

The word 'Yes', said abruptly, can mean: 'What do you want? You are interrupting me.'

If the word 'Yes' is slightly drawn out, as in y-e-e-s, it can mean: 'I am enthusiastic about that, I agree with you.'

If the word 'Yes' is very drawn out with an obvious questioning tone then it can mean: 'I am listening to you, carry on, but I am not in total agreement about your last comment.'

If the word 'Yes' is transformed into 'Yeah', it can mean: 'You're kidding, I do not believe you for one moment.'

Needless to say, if we can transform the meaning of words by how we say them, then whole sentences can be transformed with quite complex meanings and double meanings.

Do we believe the body language or the words?

Actually, this is a good question. What we tend to do is interpret what people are saying with reference to their body language. We listen to the words that people utter but we also 'listen' intently to their body language as well. *It is the body language that conveys the meaning, feelings, attitudes and emotions of the other person.*

This can be seen in the fact that, when we are speaking, we look at the person who we are talking to about 40 per cent of the time, but when we are listening, we look at them 75 per cent of the time. We have learned to observe and interpret the messages that the speaker is conveying to us non-verbally.

It is here that we must state a cautionary note. Many postures and gestures have clear meanings, but we must *always put them in context*. It is well known that when people tell lies, or even when they hear lies, that they are prone to touch their nose with their fingers or hands.

Does this mean that security staff at the airport checkout should arrest all those who, for whatever reason, inadvertently touch their nose? If this were the case, the prisons would be full of innocent people.

Even when you put the body language into context you still cannot rely on it. Non-verbal communication tends to be exhibited *in clusters* – one non-verbal message is seldom sufficient. A person who is not telling the truth, for example, may exhibit a cluster of gestures and postures, such as nose-touching, looking down or looking away, certain eye movements, sitting rather rigidly or moving around in their seats, or certain facial expressions. It is these clusters that give the game away.

Body language, as has been suggested, adds that other dimension to the words that are uttered. Body language provides the meaning and feeling to our communication. However, all of us tend to be selective in the words we use; we are not totally honest to others or with ourselves when we communicate. Social life would be very difficult if we didn't sometimes hide our true feelings and emotions, especially in the world of business. Also, none of us has a complete understanding of our own feelings and emotions, but these hidden feelings can be exhibited in our body language.

This is where an understanding of body language can help us understand ourselves, and others, because in very many cases body language *'leaks' out our true feelings*. Our emotions can be seen, not in the words we use, but in the way we say them, our head movements, our posture and so on. It is easy for someone to lie in terms of the words they use, but the truth often 'leaks' out in their body language.

We can conclude, therefore, that body language can often be more truthful of the 'real situation' than the selected words that people use. We will discuss more on this subject in the chapter on deception.

How do we know that body language conveys meaning?

The meaning of the communication is the response it receives. We have already said that most of the meaning in a communication is conveyed through the body language and not the words. Try this experiment: tell someone off with a large grin on your face and notice that the person responds to your grin and not to the words you use. In this example, the body language behaviour was not congruent with the words used and it is the body language that is believed.

Most people are unable to hide their true feelings and meanings because it 'leaks' out in their body language. Someone who is sad or upset and tries to hide their feelings with a smile will find that the 'falsehood' in their 'smile' is often detected by those around them.

When we are unable to see the person we are speaking to, such as in telephone conversations, we are deprived of the body language cues to meaning and, in these situations, we rely more on their para-linguistic cues. When you listen to your colleagues on the phone, you often know who they are talking to by their speed and tone of voice: indeed, they often mimic the other person in a subconscious way. This mimicking is often a subconscious way of establishing rapport with the other person.

If you show pictures of people exhibiting certain gestures, postures and expressions, the observer can tell you how they are likely to be feeling or what mood they are in. Clearly, a sad face indicates sadness and a happy face indicates happiness and so on.

The mood or feelings that people have, such as *anger*, *frustration*, *excitement*, *sadness* or *dejection*, *thinking* and *accusing* can often be identified in people's posture and posture alone.

Depressed   Rejecting   Excited

Defensive   Thoughtful   Confident

Figure 1.1: Body postures expressing mood and feeling

It is also interesting to note that when people talk about emotions and feelings, they use words that refer back to the body. We could make a whole list of words and phrases that link the emotion or feeling to some body posture or gesture or facial expression. Here are a few:

- **Down in the mouth** – Sad people tend to let their bottom jaw sag.
- **Laid-back** – Relaxed people or people who do not have cares tend to have a very open and relaxed posture.
- **Depressed** – Very sad people tend to lower their height and not stand upright; they are depressed or made smaller.
- **Uptight** – Tense people tend to hold themselves rigid or tight.
- **Upright** – Honest people tend to stand tall with their shoulders back.
- **He is straight** – Again, honest people stand with their backs straight.
- **He is bent** – Devious people may bend and creep around others; they lower their height. Perhaps this is where we get the expression 'creep' from.
- **He is head and shoulders above the rest** – Those who have leadership skills, or are charismatic, stand out because others lower their height around them. Whether we like it or not, we tend subconsciously to bow to those in authority.
- **Open-handed** – Honest people tend to turn their hands palms up, it is an expression of doubt or honesty.
- **Shifty** – People who are not telling the truth may shift or move around in their seat.
- **Stiff upper lip** – Holding your emotions back. Stopping your body language leaking your true feelings.
- **Tight-lipped** – Not opening your mouth, not saying anything.
- **Raised a few eyebrows** – When people hear something surprising or alarming they raise their eyebrows.

- **He/she is the right-hand man** – Supporters of powerful people are often allowed to sit on the right-hand side of the master, where they can be influential.
- **He/she is two-faced** – Cannot be trusted because they say one thing but their body language (the other side of their 'face') conveys something else.

If we spoke in a monotone and did not convey any body language but just looked blankly at the other person, they would find it very difficult to understand us. To some extent the words would be meaningless to those who were listening.

You can try a little experiment. When you are next listening to a friend talking about his or her last holiday, just look at them with no expression or body movement. Do not add any words or non-verbal sounds, just look in their direction or even look down. First of all, you will find this difficult to do and rather embarrassing and, secondly, the person who is recounting their holiday will soon stop talking and lose interest in wanting to tell you about it. It is clear from this experiment that body language is an essential part of the communication process.

When we write we exhibit body language in the form of *punctuation*. The question mark indicates the questioning tone; the exclamation mark is a mark of emphasis. The full stop separates statements and the comma indicates shorter pauses. Let us look at an example of a statement where there is no punctuation, that is, no body language.

Whether you say it, or write it, the statement is very confusing.

Dear John I want a man who knows what love is all about you are generous kind thoughtful people who are not like you admit to being useless and inferior you have ruined me for other men I yearn for you I have no feelings whatsoever when we're apart I can be forever happy will you let me be yours Gloria.

Now let us put the body language in (the punctuation).

Dear John,

I want a man who knows what love is all about. You are generous, kind, thoughtful. People who are not like you admit to being useless and inferior. You have ruined me for other men. I yearn for you. I have no feelings whatsoever when we're apart. I can be forever happy. Will you let me be yours?

Gloria

Now, of course, it all makes sense. We have included the body language and the meaning is clear.

If, however, we say the whole thing in a different way using *exactly the same words* but different punctuation, or body language, we get the following:

Dear John,

I want a man who knows what love is. All about you are generous, kind, thoughtful people, who are not like you. Admit to being useless and inferior. You have ruined me. For other men, I yearn. For you, I have no feelings whatsoever. When we're apart, I can be forever happy. Will you let me be?

Yours, Gloria

Intuition

We have all heard people use the word 'intuition' and 'intuitive'. Indeed, we have all heard the expression 'women's intuition'. The word implies some form of extra sense or extra insight into what is going on in the social world around us.

Why do we use the word 'intuition' and where is it derived from? Intuition may be due to experience, prejudice, mood etc., but most of it comes from our subconscious awareness of body language.

If someone says, 'I used my intuition, so I knew she was lying', what actually transpired was that the individual they were talking about said one thing but their body language said another. The observer put this down to their intuition, when in fact they were very observant at a subconscious level to the other person's postures, gestures, facial expressions, eye movements and so on.

In the selection interview we often hear interviewers say, 'I should have listened to my intuition, I felt he was wrong for this job and now it's proved to be the case.'

An intuitive person is just very good at interpreting body language. They do have an extra gift but it can be explained in rational, scientific terms.

What do you understand by the term 'women's intuition'? Unfortunately for men, there is some research that suggests that women are better at interpreting body language than men. This could be due to women being socialised to be more sensitive to others, or it could be that women have to be more cautious in 'mate selection', so the female of the species has evolved the extra skill of interpreting body language. It may well be that women do have more 'intuition' than men!

In effect, 'women's intuition' really means that women are better at interpreting body language than men; they do have an extra skill, but it is not some mystical female trait.

How NLP contributes to understanding body language

Neuro-Linguistic Programming (*NLP*) is a body of knowledge relating to how people perceive their world and react to it. It involves taking in information through our senses of sight, sound, touch, smell and taste, interpreting the information and acting on it.

NLP originated in the mid-1970s, when the co-founders Richard Bandler and John Grinder, with contributions from others, brought together the disciplines of linguistics, psychology, programming and modelling to form the basis of NLP. It is now an established body of psychotherapy and techniques that help people to understand their reactions to their world and to make positive changes in how they think and respond to situations.

The *'Neuro'* element refers to our neurological system of nerves that receive information from our environment and transfer messages to and from our brain, and includes our memory cells that store our memories.

The *'Linguistic'* element refers to the language we use to understand and interpret our world, communicate with ourselves through self-talk and communicate with other people through speech.

The *'Programming'* element refers to the internal programmes we create in our minds and bodies that cause us to respond to similar stimuli in similar ways. These programmes are learnt through our life experience, are mostly outside our conscious control and form the regular patterns of our behaviour. For example, do you have to think consciously about how to put on your clothes in the morning or do you just seem to do it without thinking about it? The part of your mind that is outside your conscious control (usually referred to as the *unconscious* or *subconscious mind*) takes care of the job for you, whilst your conscious mind is thinking and making choices about other things, such as what to have for breakfast.

By observing people's behaviour through their body language, you can work out what is going on in their minds, what is important to them and, over a period of time, you are likely to become skilled at predicting their reactions and responses to situations. This puts you in a powerful position, as you will be able to use your knowledge of their likely responses to situations to your advantage. For example, if you become aware that a person has an adverse reaction to taking risks, you can use this knowledge by pointing out the dangers of pursuing a course of action that you do not agree with and communicating how a way of proceeding that you prefer is a much safer option.

Representational systems

People learn to deal with their world in different ways and process information based on their preferences for using the three main representational systems of *visual* (seeing pictures and images), *auditory* (hearing sounds and noises) and *kinaesthetic* (experiencing tactile sensations and emotions). The representational systems of *taste* and *smell* often create emotional responses, so they are usually considered within the kinaesthetic category.

People who are more visually orientated often use visual words in their language, such as: *appear, aspect, bright, clear, distinguish, focus, illustrate, insight, look, observe, outlook, perspective, reveal, scene, scope, see, show, sight, survey, vague, view, visualise, watch, witness* etc. With these people, their eyes will often be upward orientated; they usually speak fairly quickly; their breathing is often shallow and confined to the upper part of their chests; and they may display excitable behaviour.

People who are more *auditory orientated* often use auditory language such as: *amplify, articulate, ask, audible, chord, communicate, compose, discuss, divulge, enquire, harmonise, hear, listen, loud, noise, report, ring, rumour, shout, sound, speak, talk, tone, vocal, voice* etc. With these people, their eyes will more often move laterally rather than up or down; they usually speak at a moderate rate; their breathing is normally full and regular from the lower part of their chests; and they do not become easily excited.

People who are more kinaesthetic orientated often use kinaesthetic and emotional language, such as: *active, affected, carry, cold, concrete, emotional, feel, flow, grasp, handle, hassle, hold, impact, motion, pressure, smell, strike, support, tangible, taste, tension, touch, unsettled, warm* etc. With these people, their eyes will often be downward orientated; they usually speak fairly slowly; their breathing is often slow and deep from their abdomens; and they are unlikely to display excitable behaviour.

You can assess the person's preferred representational system by observing and listening to them and detecting their preference by the words they use; the predominant direction of their eyes; their rate of speaking and breathing; and their general orientation from excitable to laid-back.

To gain influence over people using acceptable means, you need to establish rapport with them. This can be achieved by using visual, auditory or kinaesthetic language that matches the preferred representational system of the person; matching their rate of speaking and their general orientation from excitable to laid-back.

Rapport

Modelling behaviour is a core concept in NLP and establishing rapport with someone is a good example of modelling in action.

Rapport occurs when two people are in tune with each other and there is a high level of agreement between them. Rapport is about focusing on what we have in common, not the differences between us. The highest level of rapport occurs when you realise that the other person is communicating your own thoughts and feelings to you. At the working level, rapport means being similar enough that the differences between you do not matter.

To establish rapport between two people, it has to be worked at. It involves taking the time and effort to understand the other person's model of their world, to respect it and to make the effort to show that you understand them. You achieve this through the process of *matching* their words, tone of voice and body language, in subtle ways so as not to be accused of mimicry. You can also *mirror* their body posture by making your body posture an exact mirror image of their body posture, but be aware that you run a greater risk of being accused of mimicry when you do this.

With friends, we naturally sit or stand in similar ways; speak using similar phrases, tone, pace and volume; and adopt similar body postures. We also increase rapport when we communicate similar values, beliefs and desires.

Whilst opposites do attract – usually for a short period of time – we generally like to be with people that are like ourselves. This is because we feel comfortable and safe in an environment where we know we will be accepted for whom we are and our views will generally be supported.

Rapport then, is about focusing on the things we have in common and not the differences between us. When we want to create rapport, we value the strengths of the other person and try to overlook or make allowances for what we consider their weaknesses.

To be a 'rapport expert', you need to have good observation skills and the willingness and ability to get into the other person's world. You need to demonstrate great flexibility of behaviour if you are attempting to get into rapport with people who have very different approaches to life.

To be an excellent communicator, you will need to match the other person's language patterns, key phrases, voice characteristics, postures, gestures, feelings, values, beliefs, goals and model of the world. Not an easy task – and that is why there are so few excellent communicators. Those that do practise and acquire the skill become extremely influential people. Good actors, impressionists, politicians, leaders, teachers and counsellors have usually taken the time and effort to learn these skills.

Rapport is achieved when the other person feels comfortable with you and becomes more willing to accept your point of view. Two people in rapport will communicate in a similar way and will approximately match their body language.

If you do not have rapport then you need to match the other person's behaviour until it is established.

To test for rapport, alter your body posture and notice if the other person alters their posture to approximate yours. If this occurs, you can be reasonably sure you have a fair degree of rapport and the other person will be receptive to your messages.

Figure 1.2: Rapport process

Eye movements

When people process information, the movement of their eyes provides clues to the internal body states they are accessing:

- **Upward movements** indicate accessing *visual information* such as pictures. Eyes looking straight ahead and defocused into the distance also indicate visualisation.
- **Lateral movements** indicate accessing *auditory information*, such as words and sounds.
- **Downward movements** indicate accessing *feelings* and *emotions* or *internal dialogue*.

The meaning of eye movements is further divided into left and right movements. For most people, upward or lateral movements to the right, when looking at the person, usually indicates *recalling* information from past experience. Similar movements to the left usually indicate *constructing* pictures and words prior to speaking. Downward movements to the right usually indicate the person is undergoing *internal thought processes* for the purposes of evaluation and/or decision-making. Downward movements to the left usually indicate the person is undergoing an *emotional response* to their thought processes.

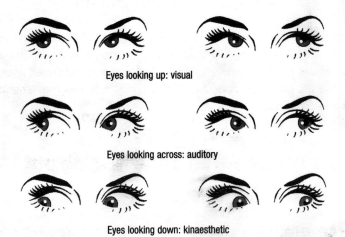

Eyes looking up: visual

Eyes looking across: auditory

Eyes looking down: kinaesthetic

Figure 1.3: Meaning of eye movements

The eyes in Figure 1.3 show the orientation of eye movements that you see when looking at the other person. For a minority of people the orientation is reversed left to right, so you need to check out their orientation before reading their eye movements. To do this, ask questions that will require 'recall' responses and note in which direction the eyes *first* move, as this will indicate their recall orientation. It is most important to be looking at the person as you ask the question, because the first eye movement is often instantaneous and then the eyes move to other orientations as they consider their reply.

Detecting lies

When you are sure of the 'recall' and 'construct' orientation of the eyes, you can use this information if you become suspicious that the person is telling lies. If you ask a question that requires recall of information and the eyes do not move to the recall orientation, the person may be lying. Check this out with further questions and look for other confirming body language indicators of lying, such as an increase in hand-to-face gestures; reduced range of vocabulary and voice tonality, reduced facial expressions and hand gestures; and change of skin colour in the face and neck area.

Be aware that some people are inclined to look directly at the person they are conversing with and eye-accessing movements may not be obvious. This may also occur if the person is suspicious of the motives for being questioned. However, most people are only able consciously to control their eye movements for a short period of time.

Do I really need to know about body language?

In normal everyday life the answer to this is 'No'! You are already a body language expert, you understand and interpret what people have to say and you are likely to have all the social skills necessary to keep your friends and have a successful social and business life.

Should you stop reading this book then? The answer again is 'No'!

There are two reasons why you can benefit from reading this book.

First, understanding body language in greater depth is itself inherently interesting. Having a fuller understanding of the social world around us makes life much more entertaining. Also, let us be honest, many of us are very nosey (another body language term) and it is great fun to find out in more detail what people are up to. Having read this book you will never sit in a bar or restaurant and be bored again, people-watching is a great pastime.

Secondly, this book is written for those in the world of work, especially for managers and leaders. We may be highly gifted interpreters of body language in our social life but the world of work is different. The world of work presents us with many artificial social situations. Very few of us have been socialised to give presentations to an audience of 50! Few of us have been socialised to manage formal business meetings! Few of us have been socialised with the skills of selling! Neither have we been socialised to make us brilliant at selection interviewing or appraising staff! We have often been thrown into these work roles and situations and a fuller understanding of body language can be an advantage to us.

The aim of this book is to enhance your skills in the work situation, to make you better at running a meeting, at giving a presentation, at selling, at selecting, and at identifying deception.

INSTANT TIP

We understand people's feelings, meanings and emotions through their body language – always put their body language into context and look for patterns of behaviour.

How can body language help me understand power and office politics?

Can an understanding of body language give us an insight into the political dialogue that goes on between people in organisations?

As we shall discover in this chapter, the answer to the question above must be in the affirmative. Power is expressed between people by subtle, and in some cases by not so subtle, means and this very often manifests itself non-verbally. In essence, people in organisations seldom come out with the blatant statement that they are superior or more important than others, but they do express this superiority by posture, gesture and tone of voice. This chapter is about the political manoeuvrings that go on between people as they struggle for power, status, wealth, influence and scarce resources.

...put things into context and define some of the terms ...going to use in this chapter. We use the term 'politics' to ...er to all aspects of influence, power and control. No organisation is without a 'political' dimension, be it pleasant or unpleasant.

'Power' is the ability to influence, control or persuade people by any means available. Power can range from subtle influence to the use of violence. In social and organisational life, power is usually socially constrained, so that violence or brute force is forbidden. The socially acceptable form of power that we find in organisations is usually referred to as *authority*. Those who exercise power over others by legitimate means are exercising authority.

Most organisations have a hierarchy of management to structure the exercise of authority throughout the levels. Not only is there a whole system of *authority relationships* between people, there is also a system of *status relationships* as well. These power and status relationships tend, over time, to establish some form of balance or equilibrium; this can be described as the 'social ecology' of organisational life. Needless to say, the social ecology of any organisation can soon be disturbed if an influential person leaves or joins, or if economic or social changes occur that causes the power and status of one department changes at the expense of other departments.

If we look at the 'social ecology' of organisational life, then we can probably describe it as a constant dance between people in their struggle to hold on to or increase their power and status over others. Managers may be constantly trying to 'control' employees, be constantly vying with each other for resources and trying to look their best in front of senior managers in the organisation. We may not like this 'political' dimension to organisational life, but it exists whenever groups and teams work with each other. The most obvious form of power is between managers and subordinates – how do managers get employees to perform according to the needs of the organisation?

In this chapter we will use the term power to refer *mainly* to socially acceptable power or what is referred to as *authority*. We will use the term power because it does not exclude the fact that in organisational life some individuals do exercise power over others that is not socially acceptable. It is not socially acceptable to exercise power over others by the use of harassment, victimisation, threats, bullying or force, but such illegitimate means are quite common in working life, especially in their subtle and non-verbal forms.

It may also be worthwhile looking at the term 'management'. Management is about 'control'; it is the control of people and resources. The word control is used here in a neutral way because there are pleasant as well as unpleasant ways to control others. Motivating your staff is a pleasant way of controlling people, so is encouraging them to achieve their targets, using money and giving rewards. The threat of disciplinary procedures is also a method of control.

Over the years, especially in Western Europe and the USA, there have been many laws and codes of practice which prevent managers and directors from exercising unacceptable methods of control over employees and each other. Needless to say, physical force and violence are illegal and there is an emphasis these days in empowering employees; *facilitating* is much more an acceptable word than managing; *consulting* is more prevalent than *telling*. So, has 'force' disappeared from organisational life? The answer could be that force and threats are seldom verbally used and seldom used in writing, but they certainly come out in people's body language and the para-linguistic cues. *It is not what they say but the way that they say it!*

Scenario

Let us look at an everyday piece of office behaviour. A subordinate knocks on the boss's office door and is asked to enter. But what is the real meaning behind this behaviour? If we observe this scene carefully we may identify how the boss subtly uses body language to accentuate his authority and keep the subordinate 'in their place'.

Subordinate knocks on boss's door. The boss makes the person wait for a quarter of a minute before saying, 'Come in!'

(Hidden message: 'I am the boss and you can wait until I am ready, because you are less important than me.' The words 'come in' are also said with impatience or annoyance, the message is clear: 'I am the boss and I do not like to be disturbed.')

The subordinate opens the door and walks into the boss's office – in body language terms the boss's territory. The subordinate may well walk slowly forward clasping both hands together in front of themselves at waist level.

(This hand-clasping is a common gesture when people enter other people's territory; it is a mild defensive gesture. In some cases, men in particular will use one hand to touch the cuff link or cuff of the other hand, this again is the same defence mechanism when entering other people's territory.)

The boss does not look up to see who it is but keeps writing or using his computer.

(Message: 'I am the boss, if you knocked on my door you must be unimportant.')

About halfway between the door and the boss's desk the boss looks up and tells the subordinate to go back and either close the office door or leave it open. (Message: 'I am the boss and can tell you to do trivial things.')

The boss again looks down and continues to make the subordinate wait until he is ready. (Message: 'What I am doing is more important than you.')

Finally, the boss looks up unsmiling and just says, 'Yes?' or 'So! What do you want?'

By now the poor subordinate has probably forgotten what they came in for, or is a nervous wreck – they actually 'feel' like a subordinate the boss has made his or her point.

If we merely wrote down the words used, they would seldom indicate the subtle aspects of the boss/subordinate relationship. We may well have the embryonic signs of bullying but none which would stand up in an industrial tribunal. Scenes like this are acted out every day in organisational life: gestures, postures, pauses, tone of voice, eye movements and head movements are used to keep people in their place.

Body language is very political!

How managers acquire power and use it non-verbally

Some early research by French and Raven (1960) has given us a very useful model to identify where managers get their power and authority.

French and Raven saw 'social power', or more correctly 'authority', as being derived from five basic areas, which they described as: position power, coercive power, reward power, expert power and referent power. These five forms of power are constantly manifested in the lives of managers and in organisational life:

- **Position power** = who they are, their position in the organisation.
- **Coercive power** = how tough they are, use of threats.
- **Reward power** = how supportive they are, the rewards they can give subordinates.
- **Expert power** = how informed they are, technically or managerially.
- **Referent power** = how unique they are, their personality or charisma.

Position power

This is the minimum form of power that a manager or team leader has, because power or authority resides in the job title or position the individual is allocated. It is interesting to note that many job titles indicate positional status such as the Foreman (meaning 'first man'), or the Supervisor (one who *looks* (visor) over others from *above* (super))

Because position power is the minimum form of power that a manager might have, it is often associated with symbols of status such as a uniform, an office or a company car. Subordinates will obey managers out of respect for the title, not necessarily respect for the individual.

Apart from the trappings of position power, such as the uniform and the office, we can often see the power relationship between the manager and the subordinates manifested in their respective body language.

The manager may adopt power postures, in this case the manager may stand with *arms akimbo*, hands resting on hips with elbows out, indicating who is in charge.

Another common posture has been referred to as the '*posture of superiority*'. In this case the manager may sit with his legs in the *cross four position* (one ankle resting on the knee of the other leg) and, in addition, he may cup his hands together behind his head with his elbows out.

Figure 2.1: Posture of superiority

One can often find two managers of similar status power both sitting together exhibiting the posture of superiority, trying subconsciously to 'out power' each other.

(In the example above we referred to male managers. This was deliberate, because female managers are less likely to use the posture of superiority as it is too overtly sexual, especially if a dress is worn. It is a very masculine posture.)

In addition to adopting these common body language postures, the manager who has position power may also resort to the scenario described above where the manager makes the subordinate wait before entering his or her office. *Pauses* in conversations are powerful ways of getting the message across, as we shall see when it comes to discussing negotiating skills.

Another expression of superiority is for the manager to look down on subordinates by tilting his or her head up and '*looking down his/her nose* at them'.

Those in power might even be seen to '*strut*' around the office, walking in a way that indicates superiority or power.

It is also interesting to note that a gesture of superiority, or an exercise of power, is to *open the door* for someone. The person opening the door, to let another person through, is indicating his superior position. We have deliberately use 'his' in the last sentence because this '*power play*' can be seen amongst men, but in many cultures it is the custom for men to open the door for women. This gesture should be seen more to do with custom and practice than an attempt to get one over a colleague! Again, we must stress that body language must be put into context.

What if a manager has no authority apart from his or her position?

If a manager has no authority, other than his or her position, then this can often be seen in the body language of the subordinates. The subordinates do not respect the person, only the position, so when the manager tells the subordinates what to do they may well obey but they may indicate to each other their resentment about this manager *who has yet to develop leadership skills.*

This rebellious body language can be seen in the *slight upward tilt of the head* with a *'tut' sound*, *eye-rolling* and perhaps even *walking away* before the manager has completely finished talking. Another indication of rebellion is to walk into the manager's office as if the subordinate owned it and it wasn't the manager's territory. It is unlikely that the subordinate would *sit on the boss's desk*, as this would be very insulting. Sitting on the boss's property and invading the boss's personal space would be doubly insulting.

Nothing is actually said – nothing that would end up in a tribunal – but an indication that the subordinate resents the 'position' power that the manager has. In the military, this is often referred to as 'dumb insolence'. Nothing is said, but everyone gets the message.

It is possible that if a manager had only the authority of his or her position but manifested the body language of superiority such as *strutting*, *arms akimbo*, *looking down their nose* etc., then subordinates would be even more resentful. *Facial expressions*, *tone of voice*, *eye movements*, *head tilts* and *curled lips* would all indicate the displeasure of the subordinates and perhaps even colleagues.

The future of position power

It is interesting to note that position power has become less important in recent years, especially in the USA and the UK. Position power is more manifest in Japan, France and Germany, but even here it is declining in importance. One of the reasons for the decline in position power is the growth of *empowerment*, giving more power to team members and those on the shop floor to make their own decisions.

In addition to this, the modern philosophy of management is to see managers as *'leaders'*, *'facilitators'* and *'coaches'*. That is, their power is more to do with their *'expertise'* (knowledge) or their ability to '*reward*' (motivate) employees. Flatter organisational structures have also reduced the importance of mere 'position' power.

Horizontal (expertise and reward) rather than *vertical* (position) lines of authority make for greater co-operation and commitment as well as encouraging teams to be self-managed and empowered.

At the Mars confectionery company in Slough (England), employees all wear the same uniform to diminish the importance of position power and the 'them and us' mentality. Other large corporations in the UK, such as the pharmaceutical firm Eli Lilly and the Eastern Group (formerly Eastern Electricity), have done away with the term 'manager' altogether, preferring instead designations such as 'coach', 'team leader', 'team member' and 'functional team leader' (leading more than one team).

Managers these days are expected to *facilitate*, not merely *administrate*. In the future the term manager may well disappear, as the terms foreman, charge-hand, supervisor and even inspector are slowly disappearing. *The decay in these terms means the decay of position power and the rise of reward power and expert power.*

Coercive power

Here power resides in the ability of the manager to coerce, force, threaten and cajole others into doing what he or she wants. Needless to say, this is not pleasant for the subordinate but all managers have the potential to be coercive; that is, to go down the disciplinary route or end the employee's contract of employment. In most cases, managers do not have to be overtly coercive, as employees know that even the kindest of managers could be coercive if they wished, and it is always a good idea to keep on the right side of one's manager! (We will see later that 'right side' is another body language expression.)

As a general rule, the more often managers resort to coercive measures, the more likely it is that they are poor managers and certainly not 'leaders' or 'facilitators'.

The body language of the coercive manager is well known and, as we said in Chapter 1, it is often made up of a combination of gestures, postures, tone of voice and facial expressions. Usually the coercive manager will adopt aggressive body language.

Coercive body language

- Standing too close to someone, invading their personal space.*
- Expressionless gaze.
- Ignoring subordinates, looking past them or over them.
- Longer than average gaze into someone's eyes.*
- Shouting.
- Finger-pointing, referred to as 'battoning'.
- Strutting down corridors in a way that conveys the impression that no one should get in their way.
- Turning away when someone else is talking.
- Peppering the conversation with snorts of derision, annoyance or disgust.
- Frowning or jutting the chin out.
- Clenching the fist.
- Banging the table.
- Storming off in disgust.
- Sarcastic expressions and tone of voice.
- Staring straight at the eyes for an overlong period. If done at close range, it is called '*eyeballing*' and is a very aggressive gesture.

(* We have put a star against these non-verbal expressions to illustrate the point that all gestures and postures need to be seen in context and also not to take one gesture or posture by itself but look for clusters of gestures. The two gestures highlighted could, in a different context, indicate affection and not coercion. Looking into someone's eyes and standing or sitting close to them can indicate attraction!)

Finger 2.2: Finger-pointing or battoning

However, coercive power can also be self-defeating. *Threats* (negative appraisal, demotion) and *non-verbal intimidation* (staring, invasion of personal space – see above) can mean that the manager will not enjoy a loyal and motivated workforce and will have to bear the extra cost of high labour turnover.

It is acceptable to be coercive if the situation genuinely requires it, such as firing someone for gross misconduct. A manager who has the courage to be coercive when it is required can gain the respect of the rest of the team. The team cannot fire the incompetent individual; it is the manager's job! Use coercive measures infrequently and only if the situation demands it.

Reward power

Unlike monetary rewards, psychological encouragement is often conveyed non-verbally, and very effectively, through gestures, tone of voice and facial expression.

There are many ways in which managers can 'reward' employees non-verbally:

- The longer than average handshake or the handclasp, using both hands to cup the individual's single hand.
- A pat on the back (this is where the expression comes from) to express praise or congratulations. Touching someone on the shoulder or arm is also a subtle way of rewarding, or thanking people; it also indicates rapport. (Those in the HR department may see such contact as politically incorrect but when people know each other and their motives, such touching is usually acceptable.)
- The smile, the nod and the longer gaze can all denote thanks and can be motivational.
- In a meeting, the slight nod of the head to suggest agreement, recognition and empathy.
- Some managers may even reward a loyal employee by allowing them to sit on their right-hand side in meetings. This is where we get the expression: 'He was the boss's right hand man.'
- Another expression indicating a powerful position or a reward for a subordinate is: 'He has the boss's ear.' Needless to say, sitting on the right-hand side of the boss allows the subordinate to communicate more easily with the boss, indeed, to whisper in his or her ear.

Touching others as a form of reward can be seen in some of the expressions we use such as: 'I was touched', 'I had to hand it to her', 'He got a pat on the back', and indirectly in other expressions like: 'He used some positive strokes.' Although these 'rewards' may seem insignificant, they are in fact very powerful and are often more lasting than the occasional financial reward; indeed, we often hear the expression: 'It was a small gesture but ...'

Never underestimate the importance of these small, non-verbal gestures; the expression 'small gesture' indicates that many rewards can be non-verbal or indeed just body language gestures.

Expert power

French and Raven correctly point out that we obey others if we believe they have some form of expertise. They may know more than we do, they may have greater technical knowledge, so we obey them because they are more likely to be right.

Most managers have two forms of expertise:

1. Their expertise may be professional or technical; they are qualified accountants, engineers, HR specialists etc. People obey them because of this technical or professional knowledge.

2. Their expertise is in management or leadership itself. These managers may manage other professional people who might be more up to date technically, or even be more qualified than the boss. However, they obey the boss because he or she knows how to manage others, how to get things done in the organisation and how to lead and motivate!

Body language can help give the impression of expertise, especially in the form of confidence and assertiveness, such people look and sound like an expert.

No matter how well qualified a person is, if they *appear hesitant*, *look uncertain*, *fail to make adequate eye contact*, *speak without self-assurance*, then people are less likely to follow them.

Confident experts are also selective about how they express themselves. If they lack confidence then they might say: '*I hope* you will enjoy this presentation', instead of '*I know that you will appreciate* what I have to say'. Those with a lack of confidence might comment: '*I think* that this is *most probably* the *best* answer', instead of: 'Under these circumstances *this is what we should do.*'

It is interesting to note that some academics on the radio and television come across as lacking expertise because they keep qualifying what they are saying (as academics should) and are rather hesitant and uncertain. This is a good example of a true expert not coming across as having expertise because of their body language and tone of voice. It is often the case that more confident people with *far less expertise* come across as more knowledgeable just because of their body language.

Those with expert power have a *confident gaze* and *good eye contact*. When they want to imply facts as opposed to doubts they use the '*palms down*' hand gesture, often with both hands. This gesture implies certainty, not opinion and not doubt. The '*palms up*' gesture, again both hands, indicates doubt and uncertainty but also honesty and openness. The '*palms up*' gesture is often accompanied by the '*raised eyebrow*', indicating doubt or the non-verbal equivalent of 'I have no idea, don't ask me'.

Figure 2.3: Palms down, 'the facts are as follows!'

Turning the palms down and appearing to press down is also a way to get others to listen to you. If the expert wants the other person to stop talking he or she may *raise their hand slightly and expose their palm* to the other person and gaze at them for a moment. The gesture conveys the 'hold on a moment' message or 'it's my time to talk'. We have seen politicians use it when being interviewed on television; it even works with the most aggressive of interviewers.

Another gesture that indicates that you are in control, and considering things in a calm manner, is the '*steepling*' hand gesture. The confident person sits in a relaxed but upright posture with their fingertips touching each other but the palms apart, forming a steeple shape. This indicates that you are considering what is being said, but you are confident and in control. Actually, adopting the 'steepling' gesture is a good technique for the manager who is confronted with an argumentative or difficult colleague. It gives the impression of being unperturbed and in control.

Figure 2.4: 'I feel confident and in control'

Research in Neuro-Linguistic Programming (NLP) has shown that we can condition ourselves to succeed or fail by our thought process. By 'self-conditioning' – maintaining an internal dialogue that reinforces personal success – we can make ourselves feel more confident, thereby making us more influential.

The important point to remember is that our feelings and emotions are reflected in our body language (see Chapter 1). This being the case, if people feel more confident and more self-assured, this will come out subconsciously in their body language. They will sound like experts and, more importantly, they will have the mannerisms, tone of voice, gestures and postures of an expert. Some of the mannerisms of the expert are listed below.

To sum up the expert should:

- Use positive-sounding words and positive emphasis to convince others.
- When talking, use the palms-down gesture to convey facts and certainty.
- When sitting, use the 'steeple' hand gesture to convey the message that he or she is in control and considering things.

- Stand upright, maintain an 'open' stance and smile to convey confidence.
- Walk with an upright posture and give the impression he or she knows what you are doing and where they are going.
- Keep their head up: looking down gives the impression of uncertainty and lack of confidence.
- Maintain eye contact with others; again it indicates confidence.

Referent power or charisma

Management theorists and social psychologists have often tried to pin down what constitutes charismatic leadership. All managers would like to have such a gift and there are many books on how to be the influential leader.

Charismatic people are often said to 'have the gift of God'; that is where the word charisma comes from. Such people seem to have a 'presence' or 'aura' about them. But when we try to pin down the qualities of charisma in the charismatic person it seems to disappear.

The reason for this is that *charisma does not exist in the so-called charismatic person* in the first place. It is a quality assigned to them by others. If you saw such a person alone on a desert island they would have no charisma; if you saw them with people who did not know them they would just be part of the group. Charisma is an emergent social property, it only exists in the social setting and in fact *it only exists in the mind of the beholder*.

You may protest that surely the charismatic person does exude confidence, does have an aura, does have a presence! The answer is 'yes, but only in the minds of the followers'. So if we want to find out if a person has charisma we should look to the followers, especially the body language of the followers or believers. It is the body language of the followers that collectively reinforces the charismatic image.

We can see evidence of the self-reinforcing aspect of charisma when the so-called charismatic person enters a room full of their followers or believers. First, when the charismatic person makes an entrance, *the followers go quiet*. Often the charismatic person actually makes a dramatic entrance because they have close loyal followers, lieutenants or *disciples*, with them. It is good for a follower to be seen *close* to the revered one, so there are plenty of people who wish to associate themselves with the Managing Director or Chairman or the celebrity. So when the charismatic person enters the room there is usually a presence because his or her close followers (disciples) have *crowded around them. Close proximity* gives others the impression of a close and emotional relationship.

Not only does the room go quiet and there is a *slight commotion* as people move round the charismatic person, there is also *movement* amongst the followers as they *make room* for their leader. In addition to this, the followers may even *gaze* at the charismatic person, slightly longer than they would at a colleague. They have made space, they have gazed, they have gone quiet: sure signs of charisma.

Sometimes you hear that the charismatic person is 'head and shoulders' above the rest. This is an interesting body language expression because it does not mean that the said person *is* taller but that they *seem* taller. This can be explained very simply by pointing out that when important people or charismatic people enter a room the rest of the people *lower their height* or *bow*. This may be very stylised as in Japan or just a subconscious lowering of the height that we find in the USA and Europe.

A few years ago, in London, we found a memo sent out to English managers in a very successful Japanese company. The memo mentioned that staff should bow when talking to superiors on the telephone. The English managers found this amusing. They commented that they would not do such a thing as it was on the telephone, and they were not going to 'grovel'. What was even more interesting is that the English managers probably did not realise that when they talk to superiors on the phone, Japanese or not, they tend to bow slightly or lower their height. Next time you see a colleague on the telephone, look at their body language and guess who they are talking to – tone of voice alone will tell you a lot. Also look at their hand movements as well as their posture; body language expressions continue even when the person they are talking to cannot see them!

Body language and leadership

If we go back to French and Raven's classification about social power, we can see that leaders may or may not have position power. If the leader is a manager or a director in the company, then clearly they have position power because of their title. Team members can have leadership skills, in that they can influence and persuade others in the team: they may not have much position power, but they may have other attributes of leadership.

Leaders may not overtly have to use coercive power but, by the very nature of their leadership, their followers want to please them and work for them, so they are exerting coercive power over others. It is highly likely that leaders have expert power as the followers want to believe that the leaders know where they are going and what they are doing. Also, by definition, leaders have reward power. Being close to the leader is rewarding in itself and one of the essential qualities that a leader has is the ability to reward or motivate others. Finally, if a manger has position power, coercive power, expert power and reward power then the followers will perceive them to be *charismatic*.

Because leadership is a perception of the followers, there are no absolute common characteristics of leaders. Leadership depends on the team, the situation and the task. A person can be perceived as a leader in one situation but not in another; a person can be seen as a leader by one group but not by another; a person can lead in one task but not in another task.

From a management perspective, the person who is likely to be perceived by the team as a leader is one who:

- Has a vision for the future; followers do not follow those who have no direction.
- Has a plan or strategy to achieve that vision.
- Can communicate the vision and strategy.
- Shows enthusiasm for the vision and strategy.
- Can motivate the team and team members.

From a body language perspective, an individual is likely to be perceived as a leader if he or she has the qualities shown above and can also look the part. Leadership requires an individual to look and sound confident and to come across as assertive.

Body language and assertiveness

Assertiveness is the ability to get what you want, or express your feelings, without violating the human rights of the other person. It is the win-win approach. We can identify the assertive approach if we compare it with the three other approaches or behaviours open to us.

There are four styles of behaviour in social and working life: *aggressive*, *submissive*, *manipulative* and *assertive*. We all use the four styles but there is a tendency for some people to use one style more than the others. In the work situation, people should be assertive most of the time, as this is the professional win-win approach.

Assertiveness basically means 'declaring your position in a firm, open and reasonable manner'. The professional manager who is 'firm, but fair' generally feels more confident.

Aggressive body language

This is one of the clearest emotions conveyed non-verbally. This is due partly to the fact that some of the gestures, postures, facial expression and tone of voice are *deliberately* formed to convey aggression. Aggression is seldom a hidden emotion, unlike manipulation or the submissive emotion. People decide to come across as aggressive; they do not usually deliberately decide to come across as submissive or manipulative. In addition, the recipient of the aggressive response has been conditioned (perhaps even genetically) to be aware of aggression, as it can be the prelude to physical aggression and violence.

Indicators of aggressive body language are:

● Clenched fists.
● Bolt upright stance.
● Presenting the side of the body slightly to get a punch in and to protect the aggressive person from being punched themselves.
● Aggressive and loud tone of voice, shouting or a raised voice.
● Finger-pointing – battoning.
● Prolonged eye-to-eye gaze (eyeballing).
● Narrowing of the eyes.
● Head-shaking in disagreement.
● Reddening of skin colour.

Manipulative body language

Manipulative body language is much more subtle than aggressive body language because the person is trying to hide the fact that they are being manipulative or devious. We associate the following words with those who are manipulative: insincere, calculating, patronising and crafty. Indicators of manipulative body language are:

- Exaggerated gestures. The open and upturned palms, held out slightly for too long and associated with an insincere smile.
- Overtly laid-back posture.
- Touching or patting in a patronising way.
- Exaggerated eye contact.
- Patronising or 'sugary' tone of voice.

Submissive body language

The individual in this case is giving away their emotional state through their body language: they want to be somewhere else. Such people are apologetic, self-deprecating and have low self-esteem. Indicators submissive body language are:

- Fidgeting and fiddling.
- Covering their mouth or eyes (perhaps they subconsciously know they are being dishonest to themselves and try to cover up).
- Slumped posture.
- Looking down or poor eye contact.
- Quiet faltering voice.
- A 'pleading', 'please like me' smile.

Assertive body language

Assertive people come across as confident, sincere, open, honest and sympathetic. If they are assertive, they respect the other person's views, even if they disagree with them they want a win-win solution. Indicators of submissive body language language are:

- Upright relaxed posture.
- Open body posture.
- Good eye contact.
- Calm and open gestures.
- Relaxed facial expressions.
- Good physical distance between themselves and the person they are talking to, not too close and not too distant.
- Unambiguous hand gestures.
- Head tilted to one side as they deliberate and intently listen to the other person (an indication of listening skills).
- Slow head nods to indicate understanding but not necessarily agreement.

The key thing about whether or not people are being aggressive, manipulative, submissive or assertive is in their attitude towards the other person and the situation. When the authors train managers in the skills of being assertive, they remind them that being assertive is made up of *three interlocking processes*. The assertive person must use the *appropriate words* – not aggressive, submissive or manipulative words. They must have *appropriate thoughts*, the cognitive element, the positive thoughts that they are right to express themselves and that they are likely to achieve the things they set out to do. And, finally, they must adopt the most appropriate *body language*.

There are two reasons why the appropriate body language is important when being assertive. First, the other person is observing the body language and, if it is inappropriate (aggressive, manipulative or submissive), then they will not believe the words that are spoken. Secondly, the appropriate body language will reinforce and create the assertive *thoughts and words*.

It seems that adopting the right postures and using the right gestures can effect how we think about ourselves and others: we can cheer ourselves up by smiling, we can feel more confident by standing instead of sitting, especially if we are sitting in a slumped manner. Body language reflects our thoughts but can also change our thoughts!

INSTANT TIP

People use body language as a way of exhibiting power, influence and control. Remember, you can only be assertive if you look the part.

03

How can body language help me uncover deception?

There are two levels in which to look at this question. First, the whole basis of the lie detector test or polygraph is based on measuring physical data such as heartbeat, temperature, pulse, etc., and this is a reasonably accurate predictor of whether or not someone is telling the truth or not. The lie detector test is used in the USA and is, at the time of writing, about to be used under certain circumstances in the UK. In this case, the physical measurements of the body actually indicate if the individual is under stress and stress is a sign that the person is aware that they are not telling the truth.

Secondly, a less accurate indicator of whether or not a person is telling lies is to watch their 'stress-related' gestures, postures and facial expressions. We pick these signals up from others, either consciously or subconsciously. In this case, we may interact with others and just feel that they are not telling the whole truth or just feel uneasy about relying on them. In many cases we do not have enough evidence about whether or not a person is lying so we just make a mental note not to trust them.

As Sigmund Freud wrote in 1905:

> 'He that has eyes to see and ears to hear may convince himself that no mortal can keep a secret. If his lips are silent, he chatters with his fingertips. Betrayal oozes out of every pore.'

Professor Ekman, Professor of Psychiatry at the University of California, has identified facial expression, gesture slips and subtle signs in speech that indicate when a person is lying. Experts trained to look out for these expressions can be quite accurate in spotting whether or not someone is lying. The most successful observers can identify lies 80 per cent of the time but, curiously, only identify truths 66 per cent of the time. However, Ekman cautions that 'judging deception from facial expressions and body language will probably never be sufficiently accurate to be admissible in the courtroom'.

Apart from the lie detector test (polygraph), used as 'scientific evidence', managers do not really need to know how accurate their perception is; all they need to be aware of is that *there is a probability* that an individual may not be telling the truth. Managers are not police detectives, judges or psychiatrists. The manager, if he or she feels that there is a degree of deception going on, can probe more deeply, follow up references, ask others about the situation and so on.

For the forensic psychologist or the police there is a need to be more certain about whether or not individuals are telling the truth. We will see some of the techniques used by the police further on in this chapter.

Telltale signs of lying

There are two things to consider when assessing whether or not people are being deceptive or not. First, people have generally been socialised to tell the truth, so even in a difficult situation, *an individual will try to avoid outright lying*. Secondly, if people are lying, they generally *show signs of stress*.

Avoiding outright lying

Let us look at the first situation, where people tend to avoid lying if they can. This can be seen in more detail in the book *Bad Lies in Business* by Comer, Ardis and Price (1992).

To avoid blatant lies, people will often do one or more of the following:

- **Fail to answer the question asked** – This is a useful ploy used by politicians who either cannot be open, or cannot commit themselves or are just avoiding telling the truth (lying).
- **Pretend not to understand the question** – Either they answer a different question that they hoped would be asked or they ask for the question to be repeated to give them time to think of a deceptive answer.
- **Remain silent** – Lawyers are always telling their clients to remain silent because they do not want their clients to condemn themselves.
- **Feign emotion** – This is a good technique to put the investigator off. As Shakespeare wrote: 'The lady doth protest too much.' In this case, the deceptive person may feign anger or resentment.
- **Pretend they are feeling ill** – Either the deceptive person pretends to be ill so they are not put under pressure or the fact that they are under stress may make them feel ill.

Bad Lies in Business goes on to suggest that if people cannot use the techniques above they will resort to:

- **Inventing a scenario** – To disguise the lie or coming up with excuses and complicated explanations.
- **Telling a tall story** – Coming up with a story about what they were doing or where they were that is fictitious.
- **Telling a lie** – The blatant untruth.

We have said that people will try to avoid the blatant lie, but *even if they are lying they may try to water down the lie* so that it does not seem to be a total untruth in their own eyes. A very good example of this is Richard Nixon's famous counter to the allegation that he authorised the Watergate break-in – he commented: 'The President would not do such a thing.' By depersonalising the act – taking the 'I' out of the equation – he absolved himself of responsibility for it.

In a similar way, President Clinton said: 'I did not have sexual relations with that woman.' This was less of a lie in his own eyes because he re-defined what he meant by sex (it wasn't full sexual intercourse) and he did not mention the woman's name. Perhaps he was thinking of women in the USA with whom he hadn't had sex!

The body language of deception

We said earlier on that feelings, emotions and attitudes are often exhibited non-verbally and that these non-verbal gestures, postures, voice inflections etc. add value to the words people use. In many cases when people are not telling the truth, the *words say one thing but the body language conveys a different message*, this is what we refer to as '*leakage*'. The most common one is when an individual says *they agree with you but their head shakes slightly*, indicating disagreement. In general, the advice is to believe the body language. Again, we should add a word of caution, as one gesture or posture is not necessarily a sign of deception; the real give-away is a *cluster* of gestures, voice intonations, and facial expressions.

A classic example of this is nose-touching, a common gesture that is often linked to deception. If, in a conversation, a person touches their nose it may be they are trying to cover up something or it may be that they have an itch or have a cold. Always put the nose-touching in context and also look for other leakage signs.

Eyebrows, forehead and face – the telltale signs

Paul Ekman has concentrated a lot of his research into facial expressions and has noted that a person's true feelings can *leak out via unconscious facial expressions.*

First, the true feelings may leak out in what can be described as a '*fleeting expression*', that is, the true feeling seems to flash across the face of the deceptive person. This would be common if someone was trying to hide their anger or their depression. I am sure we have all seen these fleeting expressions, or micro-expressions, and taken a cautionary note of them. In an appraisal situation, an individual may say they are happy with the feedback they received or that they are not really worried *but the fleeting expression indicates that they are worried.* These fleeting expressions can be so brief that they may only be picked up at a subconscious level. The observer or manager may just be left with an uneasy feeling.

A more common facial expression is the '*suppressed expression*'. In this case the person tries to cover up their true feelings with the *fake smile*, or the *fake expression of concern*; they are suppressing their real emotions and feelings. The suppressed expression comes out occasionally and usually for a longer time than the fleeting expression.

There are facial muscles that are less easy to control according to Ekman, and he calls them *'dependable' facial muscles*; they are more dependable for revealing a person's true feeling to the observer. Some of these dependable muscles are situated in the forehead and round the eyebrows.

The *betrayal of sadness* can be seen when *wrinkles appear in the middle of the forehead* because the inner corners of the eyebrows have risen. Other postures and gestures may not follow the same feeling: it has only leaked out via the forehead.

If the *eyebrows rise and come together*, this may indicate a *hidden fear* or a *hidden worry* – a useful indication when a manager is conducting a counselling or coaching session and the individual is trying to cover up their worry or fear.

Hidden anger can be seen if the *lips become narrow* and the *eyebrows are pulled downward and inwards*. Many of these subtle deceptive facial expressions are described by David Lambert in his book *Body Language* (1996).

The eyes have it!

With reference to eyes, Police interviewers are likely to have been trained in Neuro-Linguistic Programming (NLP) techniques and will observe suspects' eye movements during questioning; they are looking for the *eye accessing cues*. We observed in Chapter 1 that visual thinkers' eyes move upwards and to the right or left, auditory thinkers' eyes move laterally and kinaesthetic thinkers' eyes move downwards.

The police ask the suspect questions about where they were on the night in question and to picture where they were. *If their eyes move to the top right they tend to be remembering where they were. If their eyes move to the top left then they are constructing an image* (eye movements are reversed for some people). To the trained observer, there is a probability that, when the suspect's eyes move to the top left, they are creating or constructing an image and not remembering an image, therefore they could well be lying. If the eyes move to the top left, then the police probe more deeply because the image is being created and not brought back from the visual memory. Needless to say, the eye movements, as with a lot of body language, only give a *clue* to probable deception; it is not *evidence*.

Smiles

We are all aware of the difference between the genuine smile and the social or 'cocktail party' smile. The genuine smile expresses delight and humour whilst the social smile is 'put on' for the occasion. Dr Desmond Morris, in his book *Manwatching* (1978), differentiates between the two types of smile, the false smile and the genuine smile.

- The false smile tends to be weaker.
- The false smile appears too quickly.
- The false smile lasts for the incorrect period of time. It is either too short and is dropped once the observer is not looking, or is too long and seems to be frozen.
- The false smile is also said to be asymmetrical. It is the crooked smile compared with the broad genuine smile, with both corners of the mouth raised.
- The false smile tends to be restricted to the mouth and perhaps one cheek. The genuine smile tends to light up the whole face including the cheeks and eyes and eyebrows.

Incomplete and disguised gestures

David Lambert (1996) notes that deception can sometimes be identified by incomplete or disguised gestures.

If a manager is asked by their superior to do something they do not really want to do, but are powerless to say no, they may indicate their feelings by an *incomplete shrug*. In this case the *shoulders might be slightly lifted* and the *palms of the hands exposed*. The message is: 'I am reluctant, but I can't really say no.'

In the case of the *disguised gesture*, the annoyed or reluctant individual may be sitting down with one hand on their knee and the middle finger pointing out along their knee. This is a disguised gesture, the real gesture indicating the emotions of the individual would be thrusting the middle finger vertically upwards to say, 'Up yours!' (Lambert, 1996). In a similar manner, an individual may conceal a two-fingered insult.

Gestures, postures, facial expressions, lying and stress

Earlier in this chapter we pointed out that for the majority of people, lying causes them stress. (Although one wonders whether this applies to psychopaths who may have no conscience and therefore would feel no stress.)

Typical stress indicators given out by those who wish to deceive, are listed below.

The face

- Making odd facial expressions.
- Feigning yawns or even real yawns.
- Avoiding eye contact.
- Exhibiting glazed expressions.

- Grinding teeth or biting lips.
- Flushing or blanching of the face.
- Sweating.

The voice

- Pausing for longer than usual, or going silent.
- Repeatedly clearing the throat.
- Speech errors.
- Alternating the pitch of the voice.
- Shortage of breath.
- Difficulty swallowing.
- Dry mouth.

Gestures and postures

- Arms and legs tightly folded in a defensive posture.
- Shifting about in the seat.
- Fidgeting legs.
- Stretching.
- Being unnaturally rigid as if adopting a frozen posture.
- Rubbing the neck or pulling the collar.
- Rubbing or pulling ears.

This is a very insightful list for the police, security staff and lawyers, as well as managers who partake in selection interviewing. Let us look at some of these in detail.

Avoiding eye contact

Those who wish to deceive may *look down at their feet* or *look away*. (There are cultural differences here, as women from some West African countries may often look down at their feet when confronted by those in authority. For those in security in ports and airports this should be taken into account.)

In some cases the deceptive person may *close their eyes* but at the same time *rub one of the eyes with their finger*. Eye-rubbing is a way of avoiding eye contact.

Hand-hiding

The most obvious example of this is children who tend to *put their hands behind their backs* when telling 'lies'. It seems they are trying to hide the hands that committed the crime! Those who are intent on deception may be subconsciously aware that their hand gestures could give them away, so they will hide their hands behind their back, *put them in their pockets*, *hold the hands together* or *hide them by folding their arms*.

Nose-touching and mouth-covering

Again, children may try to conceal a lie by covering their mouth with one or both of their hands. Adults use a much more subtle technique by *just touching their mouth* with the fingers of one hand. A very common gesture is for the deceptive person to *touch their nose with one hand*.

Figure 3.1: Mouth-covering

There are two explanations for this nose-touching. First, by touching the nose, *the mouth is being covered* and it is the mouth where the lies are coming from. Secondly, if the person is under stress, and those intent on deception are, then the skin warms up and more blood goes to the nose; it is a sensitive organ. In this case the nose may itch and get slightly bigger – this is called the 'Pinocchio effect'. It is interesting to note that some people touch their nose/cover their mouth if they think the other person talking to them is being deceptive. So, in some cases, you can see whether people believe you or not!

Figure 3.2: Nose-touching

Rubbing or pulling ears

It has been suggested that when people caress the back of their ear or pull their ear lobe this, too, can indicate deception. It seems this may be linked to a child's propensity to cover both ears when being told off. In Italy, of course, a man might pull his ear lobe as an indication that he has seen an attractive woman. Again, put these gestures into context of the culture and the situation.

Fidgeting legs

Desmond Morris (1978) suggests that *leg and foot-fidgeting* can indicate stress and deception. The deceptive person tends to control their body and hands but there is more movement going on with their legs and feet. As the saying goes: 'liken yourself unto the duck, look serene on top but paddle like mad underneath!'

Shifting around when seated or adopting a 'frozen' posture

This, again, might be linked to stress and is certainly where the body language expression: 'He comes across as shifty' comes from. The constant movement, or shifting about, is certainly due to the person feeling uncomfortable about what they are being asked. The manager may note this during an interview situation when the person is asked probing questions. The manager should be aware, however, that interviewees often feel stressed merely because of the interview, let alone being asked probing questions. In some cases the deceptive person does not want to come across as stressed or shifty and they may compensate by remaining unnaturally rigid; they seem to adopt a frozen posture. The two extremes can indicate a degree of stress or deception.

Summary

For managers who are involved in interviewing candidates, talking to sales representatives, appraising or counselling people, the ability to spot possible deception is a considerable asset. We all have the skill but much of our mistrust of people is subconscious.

We have indicated above that those who tell lies often show signs of stress. It is these physical signs of stress that the 'lie detector test' is designed to pick up. The 'lie detector test' or 'polygraph' is used in the USA and it is likely to be used in the UK in the very near future. At the time of writing, in 2007, it has been reported that insurance companies in the UK are using technology that measures the stress in people's voices. When people telephone the company to make an insurance claim, the machine is switched on and it indicates what questions cause the most stress for the claimant. If there are signs of stress then this may indicate deception so the company representative probes more deeply.

If, in the interview process, the manager feels uncomfortable about someone or 'intuitively' feels they are not being honest, then the manager should probe more and follow up references. The intuition could be prejudice and wrong or it could be they have picked up those subtle body language messages of deception.

INSTANT TIP

'He that has eyes to see and ears to hear may convince himself that no mortal can keep a secret. If his lips are silent he chatters with his fingertips. Betrayal oozes out of every pore.' Freud

04

How can body language help me in security and control?

Those who guard, control, observe or investigate, such as the police and security personnel in companies, ports and airports, are tasked with the responsibility of protecting their employers and the public. They have a helping and facilitating function and yet their presence can, under certain circumstances, appear threatening. This is especially true in airports, where in most countries these days there are armed police officers.

The role of body language in security and control

For those directly involved in security activities there is a need to balance the perception of helping people and the function of control. It is precisely for this reason that armed police officers at airports and ports must be seen to be alert and professional, yet relatively inconspicuous. Their body language must indicate this professionalism. If armed officers were to be seen chewing gum, leaning against doorways, running or shouting then this would alarm the very people they were sent to protect.

The most interesting thing about those in a role of security and control is that they have to be real experts at understanding and interpreting other people's body language. They have to be extra sensitive to those around them to assess whether things are likely to get out of control or to identify those people who are intentionally or unintentionally in the wrong place and up to no good.

During a training course a female airport security officer reported that she had apprehended a woman who was carrying drugs strapped to her body. The woman was dressed to look pregnant but, according to the security officer, her suspicions were aroused because the suspect didn't have a 'pregnant face'. Such sensitivity to detail (the language of the body) has much to do with 'intuition', or having an experienced eye for the unexpected.

A question of space

The authors have come across several situations where some security staff have been identified as having more 'incidents' than others. These security people seem to be prone to upsetting members of the public or getting involved in physically aggressive incidents. Why is it that a minority of security staff find themselves in such incidents, whereas most of their colleagues seem to be able to avoid the conflict? Security staff are trained to deal with the public and to deal with prospective criminals, so what is happening to this minority who are more likely to 'get into trouble'?

The answer to the above situation is that some of those in security roles exacerbate the situation by inappropriate body language – they inadvertently cause the incident in the first place. However, to balance this out it is true to say certain criminals have been found to be ultra-sensitive to their personal space being 'crowded' compared with normal people. In this situation, some criminals are more prone to aggression, violence and to create a scene.

Julius Fast (1978) cites research in America by Dr Augustus Kinzel, which showed that some violent prisoners, when compared with non-violent prisoners, needed more space between themselves and those around them. Such prisoners seemed to resort to violence because they felt their personal space was being invaded.

It seems that the violent group had a psychological buffer zone around them four times larger in volume than the non-violent group.

Fast (1978) comments: 'Much of what Dr Kinzel calls "the quickly spiralling character of violence between overcrowded ghetto groups and the police" may be due to a poor understanding by the police of the sanctity of body zones.'

There are two key points to consider here when it comes to body language and security and control.

First, some security officers may create an incident or generate violence because their body language is inappropriate, especially if they invade the 'personal space' of a suspect or even a member of the general public.

Secondly, some individuals are more prone to aggression and violence because they feel they need more personal space than others. Getting too close to these people invariably leads to aggression or violence.

As we shall see later, for those in security and control, it is better to maintain a physical distance between themselves and those they need to control, so as not to provoke them. This is especially true if they are to question a suspect who is prone to being aggressive or violent.

Having said all the above, there can be occasions when invading a suspect's personal space can help in the process of interrogation. This should only be done in the controlled environment of the interview room, where there is more than one member of the security team, and where any possible aggression can be controlled.

Again, Fast (1978) cites the example of the American police who deliberately interrogate suspects by sitting very close to them and making sure that there is no chair or table between them and the suspect. It seems that the chair or table would give the suspect some form of psychological barrier to protect them and give them confidence. Fast (1978) comments:

> '*the questioner, although he may start with his chair two or three feet away, should move in closer as the questioning proceeds, so that ultimately one of the subject's knees is just about in between the interrogator's two knees.*'

The effect of this invasion of the suspect's personal space seems to be to break down the suspect's self-assurance and confidence.

Airport security – high stress and low tolerance

We are highlighting airports because they are an extreme example of where security and control are very important. The issues about body language in airports can be extended to other areas of social life where security and control are important issues.

Whether you are employed in airport security and control or are merely a business traveller, the airport is a highly stressed environment. In *Manwatching* (1978), Desmond Morris found that more verbal and physical aggression is exhibited at airports, railway stations, bus stations and ports than in most other public places. Airports, in particular, are subject to high levels of such stress-related behaviour.

Even for the seasoned business traveller, going to an airport can be a stressful experience. First, there is the whole problem of worrying about missing the plane. Travelling to the airport is also a problem, because of motorways, traffic jams and general travel anxiety. Also, once you have arrived, finding a place to park the car at the airport causes tension. On top of these worries, for international flights, you have to book in several hours before take-off.

The upshot of this is that the average traveller is in a state of tension and anxiety even before he or she enters the airport terminal. Once in the airport, the problems are multiplied, as described below.

Fear of flying

Desmond Morris found that people exhibited ten times as many signs of tension (displacement activities) at airports as at railway stations. Only about eight per cent of the passengers about to board a train showed these signs, but the figure rose to 80 per cent at the check-in desk of a jumbo jet flight.

Loss of personal space

Aggressive body language arises, as we saw above, when people are forced to wait in queues, are crowded into restrictive spaces or feel crammed into aeroplane seats. In the USA and Western Europe, personal space is said to be anything under arm's length; in the Mediterranean cultures, it is under elbow length; whilst in Eastern Europe, it is about 'hand' length – that is, standing very close to people. In the airport, people from other cultures may invade each other's space in an aggressive manner without realising it.

Discomfort

Being forced to mix, in close proximity, to people from other cultures with different gestures, postures and different languages and expectations makes people uncomfortable. Queuing, for example, may be an expected form of behaviour in some cultures but not all! The British tend to keep themselves to themselves in public places like airports and stations and will talk quietly. People from some other cultures will seem loud to the British and this can create anxiety, because loud voices often signal problems and issues.

Uncertainty

People become apprehensive when time is ticking away and they are uncertain as to whether or not they are in the right queue or the right place. However, many signs there are in the airport terminal, uncertainty and confusion are very common.

Being observed and controlled

A whole host of security staff, armed police, customs and excise and other airport and airline officials will be observing and controlling. The presence of these people makes even law-abiding citizens anxious. In addition to this, high security in airports often means that passengers are forced to take off their shoes, take off their belts, unload anything metal and go through X-ray machines whilst still being anxious about missing the flight!

Fear

Finally, the fear of having forgotten something or losing something causes tension, especially essential things like passports and credit cards.

Recognising tension

It is the job of those in security and control to recognise tension in the social situations above. Being able to recognise tension in others is a first step towards limiting confrontation and alleviating stress. Because fear of flying is common amongst passengers, the cabin crew are specially trained to watch for signs of tension. The crew themselves are trained to look professional, relaxed and in control. The last thing passengers want to see is panic or fear or stress amongst those on whom they rely!

Signs of tension

- Repeatedly checking tickets, wallets and passports.
- Rearranging hand-luggage.
- Dropping things.
- Constantly making last-minute checks.
- Changing position in seat.
- Grimacing.
- Scratching the head.
- Tugging the earlobe.
- Lighting but not smoking cigarettes.
- Repeatedly breaking matches.
- Rubbing the back of the neck with the palm of the hand.
- Arms folded with the hands gripping the upper part of the opposite arm.

In some cases, the tension amongst those who are travelling manifests itself in other, more aggressive, ways. This aggression might be directed at inanimate objects, such as the airport furniture, or through slamming doors. Aggression can sometimes be targeted at other passengers or, more commonly, at airport staff, especially if there is some problem such as flight delays and cancellations.

No wonder that airport staff involved in security and control have to be extra wary when it comes to talking to people, giving them information which might be seen as negative and when involved in crowd control. The situation is fraught with difficulties.

Clearly, security staff should avoid making things worse by raising their voice, pointing, rolling eyes in frustration, and standing too close. One of the main things to avoid are hand gestures that could be seen as aggressive or rude in other cultures. The British security officer may innocently raise their open hand to stop someone but in Greece such a gesture could be interpreted as a 'moutza' or the 'go to hell' gesture.

Predicting aggression

It would be very useful for those in security and control if they could predict whether an individual was likely to become aggressive or even violent. We said earlier on that some people in security and control are involved in more conflict situations than others and it is these people who are poor at predicting conflict and/or use inappropriate body language. Some individuals are sensitive to others' body language and can see if things are likely to get out of control. These people step back and try to calm things down. What should we be looking for if we are going to predict possible aggression between people?

- Standing with feet apart, hands placed on hips or thumbs in the belt or pocket.
- Shaking a fist at another person.
- The hand used like an axe to chop or slice, in an imitation of an execution.
- Prodding with the finger tips in the direction of another person's eyes.
- Finger-pointing, especially with back and forward movements.
- Staring into the other person's eyes for a prolonged period (eyeballing).
- Crowding or invading the other person's space by standing in close proximity to them.

Predicting violence

The above expressions of body language indicate the possibility of hostility, anger and perhaps verbal aggression. Can body language help us predict the possibility of violence? The body language we saw above may well be precursors of violence, but are there other signs?

The clue to potential violence can be seen when the aggressive person starts 'adrenalising'. This is part of the body's 'fight or flight' response, caused by adrenalin being pumped round the body in preparation for action. The main signs are:

● Breathing tends to speed up and deepen.
● Sweating occurs.
● The mouth feels dry and the individual licks their lips and starts swallowing.
● Face tone turns pale.
● Shivering may begin (symptoms that Desmond Morris describes as the 'cold sweat of fear').

In addition, the body posture begins to alter:

● The body tends to 'square up' to the potential opponent, feet are placed apart as the body faces the other person.
● Eyes narrow.
● Mouth widens.
● Shoulders are raised and the neck and head are thrust forward.
● Arms tend to be slightly bent and the fists begin to clench.
● As the trunk moves forward, the abdomen contracts and the knees bend to give more 'spring' in defence as well as attack.

How to avoid conflict and violence

The aim is to use the understanding of body language to reduce the likelihood of creating situations where aggression and violence are the outcomes.

Be assertive, not confrontational or submissive. We saw earlier that people can respond in four ways: *submissive*, *aggressive*, *manipulative* or *assertive*. The assertive style is the win-win approach. Adopt an open and confident body posture, use a reasoned tone of voice and show you are considering the other person's point of view. If you are submissive in your tone of voice and body language it can bring out the 'bully' in aggressive people and make things worse. If you adopt a manipulative style and tone and the other person sees through it, this can annoy them.

Use the guidelines below to handle difficult people and situations:

- Remain calm in your tone and in your gestures and postures; you need to be seen as confident and in control.
- Keep at arm's length, because this allows you to step aside should the individual lunge at you. Never attempt to touch or grab someone who is angry, as this will encourage retaliation. You can always tell if you are getting too close to someone as they will usually step back, lean back or fold their arms in a defensive posture. The general rule is to keep a good physical distance between you and the potentially aggressive individual. As we saw in the early part of this chapter, violent people tend to want more physical space compared with non-violent people.
- Refrain from 'talking down' to the other person or using gestures that could be interpreted as you implying their stupidity. People are not stupid. They may be confused, difficult, slow, muddled or even disabled in some way, and you certainly have to give the benefit of the doubt to someone with sight or hearing limitations.
- On no account should you raise your voice. Shouting is seen as aggressive and is likely to annoy not only the person you are dealing with, but also those in the immediate vicinity.

- Avoid pointing at people, as this is perceived as aggressive. If you want their attention, or you wish to direct them in a certain way, use your whole hand. Even pointing with your thumb, nodding or tossing your head in a certain direction are regarded as surly gestures and are likely to cause irritation.

- Do not beckon with the forefinger, as this is often perceived as demeaning or sarcastic. It is better to roll all the fingers towards you with the palms up, although in Italy, Spain, South America, Africa and Asia the same gesture is used but with the palms face down. When dealing with children or large groups, it is acceptable to use the whole arm to beckon, but this should be done slowly so as to avoid the impression of rushing people. You may have noticed that tour guides and the military raise the whole arm above their heads while rotating the forefinger, meaning 'come round me'.

- Retain eye contact with the person to show that you are interested and concerned about what they are saying. Looking down, or looking away or looking over their heads can be seen as showing a lack of respect and can cause annoyance.

- If you need to say 'No' to someone, do so in a friendly manner. Do not shake your head or wag your finger; it is better to use your whole hand palms down whilst at the same time maintaining friendly eye contact.

- If you are sitting, maintain an upright posture, as this appears attentive, professional and lacking in tension. Slouching, hanging legs over chairs, or feet on desks appears disrespectful. The last thing you should do is lean back in your chair clasping your hands behind your head with elbows sticking out. This is a posture of 'superiority' and is often interpreted as a posture of 'arrogance' by others.

- Avoid 'picking lint' – picking imaginary pieces of fluff off your clothes. The effect of this gesture is to indicate that you are not in agreement with someone but you cannot be bothered to argue with them. We will see this gesture mentioned again when watching people's behaviour in meetings.

- Avoid all forms of gestures that indicate aggression, insults, superiority or lack of concern. In a multi-cultural setting it is probably wise to smile, keep your distance and avoid all hand and head gestures that could be misinterpreted.

- Above all, show understanding when the person you are dealing with is getting flustered. Simple gestures, such as patting the palms in a gentle, downward motion combined with comments such as, 'I understand your feelings, so lets talk about it', can make a difficult situation less confrontational. The age-old tradition of offering tea or coffee at such times might also work well. Once an individual has a cup of tea or coffee in their hands and is about to drink it they cannot adopt a defensive or aggressive posture.

For those people employed in security and control, an understanding of body language is an essential tool of their trade. Looking out for signs of anxiety and aggression and dealing with the situations using the techniques explained will improve your job performance and personal security.

INSTANT TIP

You may be put into difficult situations with difficult people. Be very aware of their body language; do not make things worse by your body language and, above all, do not invade their personal space.

05

How can body language help me in interviewing, counselling and feedback?

Interviewing – selection and appraisal

Figure 5.1: There is something about this candidate I do not trust

The most common form of interview is the selection interview and in this case the manager needs to get information from the interviewee so it is the interviewee who should do most of the talking. As a general rule the interviewer should do about 25 per cent of the talking; basically describing things and asking questions. The interviewee should do 75 per cent of the talking by providing adequate answers to the questions. In a counselling interview the person being counselled should do as much as 90 per cent of the talking, as the aim is for them to understand for themselves and not for the counsellor to impose a solution on them. In feedback the talking should be about equal, as both parties explore the situation and agree ways forward.

The key thing in the interview is that the interviewer should be an active listener, and active listening involves a lot of body language gestures, postures, changes in the tone of voice and non-verbal sounds. It is these active listening gestures, postures and facial expressions that encourage the interviewee to talk. In addition, the interviewer needs to observe the body language of the person being interviewed to find out whether they are being genuine or not or whether certain questions cause them to become uncomfortable.

It should be remembered at this point that, from the interviewee's point of view, their CV is a sales document. They want to get an interview, so many CV's are 'economical with the truth'.

In a survey of 1,500 companies, it was found that 71 per cent had encountered serious lying on CVs. Of the most common lies on CVs, 31 per cent were about previous experience, 21 per cent about university qualifications, 19 per cent about salary and 18 per cent about secondary qualifications (Experian Survey, *The Guardian,* 15 January 2000). Needless to say, the interviewer should be looking for signs of stress in the interview, as this may indicate lies or at least exaggerations on the applicant's CV.

First impressions

In the case of the selection interview, it is the first impression that both parties make of each other that often, irrationally, determines the outcome of the interview. Both the interviewee and interviewer should be aware of the importance of the first impression and the role body language has in creating prejudices and misunderstandings. The interviewer has to be careful not to prejudge the interviewee on the basis of the initial signals; the word 'prejudice', after all, means to prejudge. Research has shown that when we first meet others we automatically make judgements about them, such as personality, intelligence, temperament, working abilities, suitability as a friend or lover and so on.

Sometimes it is 'intuition' that informs us, in the sense that we subconsciously draw conclusions from the body language cues. We may feel we know or understand the interviewee based on how we perceive their body language and how they present themselves. These perceptions – don't forget they can also be prejudices – can be positive or negative. All interviewers have prejudices, both positive and negative, so the professional approach is to try to make allowances for them. Prejudices can be based on our perception of the other person's personality, their social class, their ethnic background, gender, dress, appearance, accent or dialect, their hobbies or interests or what sports they follow and so on.

Here are some simple rules for neutralising first impression bias:

- Be prepared to recognise your own prejudices and make allowances for them.
- Remember that assumptions about people and the odd body language cue do not constitute facts or evidence.
- Go out of your way to treat every interviewee in the same way and ask them the same set of questions so you can make comparisons. The follow-up questions you ask, based on the answers to the initial questions, can clearly vary.

The best way to get a realistic picture about how an interviewee is likely to behave in their next job is to ask them 'behaviourally-based' questions. These questions ask the interviewee how they behave in a real situation in their present job. The questioner does not start off with 'What would you do if ...' (hypothetical question) but one that asks them to think of real events or experiences they have been involved with. A typical behaviourally-based question might be: 'In your present job you have bound to have come across a difficult employee/customer; give us an example of your experience and how you dealt with it.' The interviewee is being directed to a real incident and is likely to be honest about how they actually behaved.

Establishing rapport

Whether it is an appraisal interview, a selection interview or a counselling interview, the best approach is to establish a relaxed and friendly atmosphere. It is in the relaxed interview situation that people open up and are more likely to tell you the truth. If the interviewee is stressed, they will tend to give you textbook answers to the questions and not answers that tell you how they really feel.

The interviewee is usually nervous, especially if they are very keen about the job on offer. This nervousness can get in the way of a frank and open interview so the interviewer should try to establish rapport and a relaxed atmosphere. There is some debate about not having a table between the interviewer and the interviewee: as we saw in the chapter on deception, the table can be a psychological barrier. If you were counselling someone, the table would be in the way, as you want the individual to be as open as possible. In an appraisal it would probably be best to have a small, low table, like a coffee table. In the selection interview, interviewer and interviewee probably do not know each other and so the office table might make them feel more comfortable. The interviewee, in particular, might want to hide their nervousness and may feel too exposed with no table between them and the interviewer.

Breaking the ice

Whatever the interview situation, it is best to get off on the right foot: you want the interviewee to be open, you want them to be relaxed and you want them to do most of the talking.

One method is informally and very briefly to outline the process of the interview. If it is a selection interview, then tell the interviewee you will be asking them questions about their current job or experience. If it is an appraisal interview, it is a good idea to remind them that they need to appraise themselves and identify what their development needs are and that it is your job to listen and respond. If it is a counselling interview, you will mention that your role is one of a sounding board to help them review their options and decisions. This opening should be very relaxed, with open smiles and an open body posture. If you come across as too formal, or lean forward, or don't smile, have arms and legs crossed, or adopt the posture of superiority – legs in the 'cross four position' with hands behind your head and elbows out – your postures will prevent the interviewee from opening up.

Having said all this, it is very likely that the selection interview candidate, or the appraisee or the person who feels they need counselling, will come across as being *defensive*. They may well have their *arms folded*, *ankles crossed*, *not smile* and *look tense*. Your relaxed posture and smiles should set the right atmosphere and you can informally set the scene.

Another thing you can do is say you are getting coffee or tea or another drink. If you ask very nervous people if they want a drink, they will often turn it down but if you imply that you are getting a drink anyway, and ask what would they like, they are more likely to accept it. Never underestimate the usefulness of tea or coffee to break the ice. It is a simple process; if their legs and arms are crossed in a defensive posture they have to physically change posture to lean forward to drink the tea or coffee. There is evidence to show that getting people to open up physically has the effect of getting them to open up mentally as well.

Active listening

We have mentioned active listening, using body language and non-verbal sounds, as well as encouraging words, to keep the person talking and to expand on what they are saying. Active listening should be used in selection, appraisal and counselling interviews. The active listener should sound interested, maintain reasonable eye contact and observe the other person's body language as well.

Cocking the head to one side shows you are taking in what is being said and being attentive.

Nodding the head slowly indicates you are listening (remember that nodding the head more rapidly indicates agreement). A slow head nod will encourage the other person to continue talking. One of the reasons why a single interviewer should make notes of the interview, after the candidate has left, is that as soon as the interviewer looks down to make written notes the interviewee will often stop talking. Another technique interviewers can use is to use a clipboard, so they can just tick pre-prepared boxes without losing eye contact.

Raising the eyebrows, leaning forward and a slight gesture with the hand can indicate you want to say something. Raising the hand slightly can also indicate you want them to stop what they are saying so you can add something or ask another question.

The problem with the selection interview is that you do not really want to indicate that you agree or disagree with what the interviewee is saying; if you did this then the interviewee would pick up the clues and just tell you want you want to hear. On the other hand, if you had an expressionless 'poker face' (not giving any emotions away), then the interviewee would just stop talking. In the selection interview, the interviewer should smile, nod, make encouraging sounds, look relaxed and keep the interviewee talking. But beware – there is a fine balance between the body language of encouragement and the body language of agreement!

Counselling

Many counselling sessions involve an employee who has personal problems and issues that are founded in attitudes, feelings and emotions. We found in Chapter 1 that people's body language allows us access to these emotions and feelings; we can observe that 'something is wrong' by observing the body language cues such as:

- Drooping shoulders.
- Lack of eye contact.
- A sullen appearance, as if the person has no strength or energy to smile or look up.
- Self-protective 'wrapping', in which the arms are folded in front. This can be defensive but in this situation it can also suggest withdrawal or a need to feel safe.
- Fidgeting and changing position suggests anxiety and nervous tension.

Figure 5.2: 'I'm okay – nothing wrong with me'

The counsellor's role is to get the individual with the problem or issue to open up and discuss how they see the situation. The counsellor should do a lot of active listening and use encouraging words. They should never be judgemental and they should never apply pressure to get the other person to be open and talk things through. Counselling is only fruitful if the employee discovers the solution for themselves, and this only occurs through listening and encouraging.

Counselling the stressed employee

It is the manager's role to identify those who are stressed and unable to cope. Stress could be due to work overload, poor time management, lack of experience, lack of training or some outside work factor. The trouble is that most stressed individuals are less aware of the symptoms than those around them, because they have developed coping mechanisms and are unaware of their changed behaviour. The characteristics of the stressed individual in terms of body language are:

- Hypersensitivity to mild criticism, or even helpful advice.
- Displaying tense postures, such as the hunched or burdened look.
- Showing irritation, such as shrugging of the shoulders, 'tutting' or casting the eyes to the ceiling.
- Appearing restless, even trembling.
- Nervous laughter or incoherent speech.
- Tense muscles.
- Indigestion or nausea.
- Increased heart rate.
- Aches, pains and twitches.
- Appetite changes and problems sleeping.
- Tiredness, exhaustion or even listlessness.

The key thing to remember is not to confuse counselling with giving advice. Male managers, in particular, tend to be impatient and will rush to give advice, but this seldom works because the employee needs to understand the underlying cause of their problem and advice is not what they actually need.

It is interesting to note that some physical symptoms seem to exhibit themselves when people are stressed and there seems to be a relationship between the following:

- Backache very often relates to the lack of support. Also, the depressed posture of an arched back will tend to make it ache.
- Stomach trouble can be related to the emotion of 'not being able to stomach' something.
- Tension headaches can be linked to psychological pressure.
- Breathlessness can be related to the fear of performing badly.
- Blurred vision can be linked to panic, or loss of perspective.

Feedback

If you are a manager, one of your key skills is to provide people with feedback on their performance in ways that encourages them to change their behaviour to achieve the outcomes the organisation needs. Feedback is often an integral part of appraisal and coaching processes within the organisation.

Feedback is an interpersonal skill involving an exchange of information, a willingness to listen, to learn and to modify our behaviour to achieve the outcome we are seeking.

There are no hard-and-fast rules for delivering feedback, as the circumstances in which it may be given will vary widely. However, here are ten general guidelines that will make your feedback more acceptable.

1. Readiness

Consider the other person's readiness to hear your feedback. Feedback works best when the person is ready and willing to receive it. When the person is not in the right frame of mind, the feedback may be interpreted as destructive rather than constructive. You can nearly always tell about a person's state of mind by their body language. It is often a waste of time giving feedback to someone who has adopted defensive gestures or postures.

If you detect the person is not ready for the feedback, choose another time to give it. Help the person to prepare for the feedback session by asking them to think about and prepare for the feedback meeting. Ask them to think about what aspects of their performance worked well and what aspects of their performance they could improve upon.

Some people may be so defensive that they will never be ready to receive feedback and display resistance to your attempts to deliver it. In this situation, try to provide more praise than criticism, so they lose their fear of receiving feedback and, as they become used to the feedback process, you can become more honest in your discussion with them.

As a general rule, and especially for people who are likely to become defensive or aggressive when receiving feedback, establish some ground rules in advance – such as, the person speaking will not be interrupted and the person listening will be given full opportunity to respond.

In your discussions as part of the preparation phase, use an open body posture, a friendly expression, normal voice volume and minimal gestures. Expect the other person to become suspicious or defensive. Answer any questions they may have but do not alter your body language to match their more defensive body language. Here we want the other person to see that you are displaying normal and constant behaviour and, after a short while, their body language should start to match yours as the defensiveness dissipates.

2. Self-review

Encourage self-review. Start by encouraging the person to appraise their own performance and then build on their insights. The person will be more willing to accept feedback when he or she has recognised his or her own strengths and weaknesses.

Due to our different personalities, expect people to adopt different attitudes towards a self-review of their performance.

3. Own your feedback

Wherever possible, use what you saw and heard, not what has been reported to you. Own your feedback by using 'I' statements and make it descriptive rather than judgemental. Describe what you observed without making value judgements about how right or wrong you consider the behaviour. For example, 'I often feel you do not listen to my ideas' is descriptive: 'You're not willing to listen' is judgmental.

Deliver positive feedback in friendly manner, congratulating the person on good aspects of their performance. Deliver negative feedback in a calm and factual way, maintaining good eye contact, normal voice volume and gesturing as little as possible.

Be open to receiving feedback yourself. Your actions may contribute to the other's behaviour.

4. Specific

Make your feedback specific rather than general. Concentrate on particular aspects of behaviour that need improving. It is easier for the people to react constructively to specific issues than to general statements. For example, saying, 'You are useless with customers' offers no information on what actually is wrong and is likely to give offence. Saying, 'I notice that you don't treat customers in a friendly way' is specific, less offensive and more likely to lead to an agreed solution.

5. Constructive

Make the feedback constructive by praising positive aspects and agreeing areas for improvement, rather than just concentrating on areas of poor performance. Try to avoid using negative words such as *bad*, *wrong*, *poor*, *unacceptable*, *useless* etc. These are what we call '*hot*' words and are likely to inflame the person. Instead, use less emotive and more positive words such as *develop*, *improve*, *change*, *modify*, *enhance* etc.

Explore alternative courses of action rather than providing solutions. The more you can involve the person in solutions, the more you will increase the probability of successful outcomes.

6. Achievable

Make your feedback acceptable and practical by suggesting what might be done differently and more effectively. Encourage the person to try out a different approach and evaluate its outcome. Do not ask the person to change their personality and beliefs but do ask them to change their behaviour. Tell them what they must do and also what it would be desirable for them to do. Provide coaching and/or training if needed and sufficient time for them to develop the new behaviours you are seeking.

7. Acceptable

As far as possible, give feedback that is asked for rather than imposed. If this is not possible and you must bring aspects of behaviour to the person's attention, tell them that you are giving them feedback to help them in their work.

Your feedback is only valid if it is understood and accepted. Give feedback using language and style of behaviour that will be acceptable to the person. Check for understanding and acceptance on key points. Actively listen and try to understand any response you get and help the person to appreciate your points of view. Ask questions about performance rather than making statements and, wherever possible, allow the person a choice in the actions they will take.

Do not try to make the person change their behaviour in ways that they are unable or unwilling to do, as this will lead to resistance and the opposite of the outcomes you are trying to achieve. In this situation, change the job to fit the talents of the individual better or, if this is not possible, make the person aware of the consequences of failing to change their performance.

8. Prioritise

Do not overload the person with too much information at one time. Prioritise the points that you want to discuss and focus only on what is most important, offering just enough information for the person to understand the key points you want to convey. Getting everything 'off your chest' in one go may be therapeutic for you but the person receiving this data overload is unlikely to learn from it or be willing to change their behaviour.

9. Time

Give feedback at an appropriate time. Feedback given immediately in the heat of the situation is unlikely to be well thought through, and will be poorly delivered and poorly received. Feedback should be given calmly and rationally in most situations, because people are unreceptive to information and learning if they are feeling threatened.

However, feedback stored for too long loses its impact and relevance from the other person's standpoint.

Put aside the time needed to give your feedback properly, so that the person will understand what you have said and feels they were fully able to discuss it with you.

10. Place

Give feedback in an appropriate place. Avoid offering negative feedback in public. A useful principle is to 'criticise in private and praise in public'. If the person is likely to see the feedback as criticism, then arrange somewhere confidential to give it. Try to ensure the person will not feel at a disadvantage in the place chosen to give the feedback. Remember that making a subordinate leave their working area to come to your office may be intimidating for them.

INSTANT TIP

Observe people's body language and you have the route to their inner feelings.

06

How can body language help me in meetings and presentations?

We are covering meetings and presentations together in one chapter because, in terms of body language, they are both rather formal methods of communication. In addition, the body language of the chairperson and presenter is important but so is the body language of the participants and the audience. The successful chairperson and the successful presenter should be aware of their own body language and the body language of those around them.

Meetings

Before we look at the significance of body language in meetings, we ought to remind ourselves about the benefits of running good meetings and some of the basic reasons why we have meetings.

Benefits of a well-run meeting:

● It saves time, money and repetition to bring people together to explain or discuss issues.
● If all people have the same information and have discussed issues together, they are more likely to be co-operative.
● It is a very effective method of problem-solving and decision-making.
● It can improve motivation and enthusiasm.

There are many reasons for meetings, such as:

1. **To inform** – One of the key purposes of a meeting is to inform people about business issues.

2. **To test out ideas** – A person calls a meeting to test out ideas and proposals to find out what people think.

3. **To listen** – A meeting, in this case, enables members to listen to ideas that might be valuable to them, such as from an external sales executive or supplier.

4. **To problem solve and be creative** – Groups make better decisions than individuals working alone, so a meeting to solve or brainstorm issues can be very effective.

5. **To make decisions** – To involve people in making decisions so they feel part of the decision.

6. **To agree or reject recommendations** – To make people aware of the reasons for acceptance or rejection.

7. **To air grievances or to reveal attitudes** – To provide an opportunity for an exchange of feelings about a situation.

8. **To change behaviour** – Group pressure on individuals is usually more powerful than a lecture from the boss.

It is very often the case that a meeting has an agenda that incorporates many of the above objectives, some of them overt and some of them covert.

We can find out a lot about what is going on in a meeting by looking at body language. There are two areas we should focus on, the body language of the *chairperson* and the body language of the *members*. (In the same way, when we are looking at the skills of *presentation* we are looking at the body language of the *presenter* and the body language of the *audience*.)

Body language of the chairperson

Again, we would like to remind you that body language is not rocket science and you will be aware, both consciously and subconsciously, of many of the non-verbal activities that go on in meetings. In this section we are highlighting how an effective chairperson uses body language in a meeting and what the chairperson might look out for amongst the members.

The key thing about meetings is that the chairperson and the members want as much constructive involvement from participants as possible. *We do not need reminding that a meeting in business is all about effective communication and effective communication nearly always involves non-verbal behaviour.*

The chairperson needs to be in control of the meeting and to keep people's attention on the topic being discussed. The key instrument of control, in terms of body language, is *eye contact* with the members. The effective chairperson glances *his or her eyes constantly from member to member in a random fashion*. This has the effect of allowing the chairperson to *pick up nuances of non-verbal behaviour* to assess members' feelings and attitudes. In addition, members are aware they are being watched and will maintain their attentiveness.

The chairperson can also maintain attention, and keep the focus on the agenda item, by the subtle use of the *tone* of his or her voice. If a few members have lost focus and have started a small submeeting, then the chairperson can *raise his or her voice slightly* and at the same time *gaze at the subgroup*; nothing has to be said, nothing need be said.

It is a good idea for the chairperson to *vary his or her tone of voice* so as to avoid sounding monotonous. The reason for this is that it again helps keep members' attention. This is particularly important because not all agenda items are directly relevant to all members and their minds can wander.

As with making presentations, the chairperson should use head, shoulders, arms, hands and facial expression to put over points and emphasise issues. The chairperson of a meeting need not be as animated as the person giving a presentation. However, a degree of animation means they are more likely to be seen as *believable and professional*. Being animated as opposed to being physically static is also another way of maintaining the members' attention.

As the chairperson, you should make sure everyone in the meeting has an opportunity to be involved. You should look round the group to see who wants to contribute *and ask them for their views* and using their first names, if appropriate, ask them to do so with *direct eye contact*. There are usually talkative people in meetings and quiet people. Do not let the talkative people dominate the proceedings and make sure you *involve the quiet ones*. In some cases the quiet ones have good ideas but need to be encouraged to speak out. If there are members who are apt to dominate proceedings then you could quickly *glance past them* and identify another individual to contribute. You should not be rude, but nod quickly at the talkative person indicating that other people need to contribute as well.

You should control the time spent on each agenda item. You can do this verbally or more subtly by placing your watch in front of you and using your *tone of voice* to move things on.

If you want to involve a member you should not point at them but *direct an open hand, palms up or sideways*, in their direction. As we have seen before, pointing is seen as aggressive and rude. Another use of the palms is to calm down some members who have become argumentative, *both hands, palms down, in a patting motion,* helps to calm things down and keeps you in control of the meeting.

If a member speaks for too long, or you want another member's opinion, you can *point a hand, palm vertical*, at the speaker whom you wish to curtail.

If an argument seems to be getting out of hand, you can resort to the more forceful scissor movement of hands crossing both forearms in a cutting gesture – this clearly states: 'That is enough, let's move on.'

Your role as the chairperson in the meeting should be to *enable people to express their views* in the most constructive way as possible. You should try to *refrain from using non-verbal signs of discontent or disagreement* if you really want to find out the feelings of the members; this is particularly important in brainstorming, where even crazy ideas can have some value. As a general rule, you should never tell the group your ideas first, as some members will just agree with you whatever you say.

Body language of the members

The effective chairperson will be tuned into the body language of the members of the meeting, as we shall see, these are similar in many ways to the body language of the audience in a presentation.

The chairperson should be aware of negative body language that some members might exhibit. This negative body language indicates disagreement that might need to be brought out in the meeting, and it is the chairperson's job to encourage all opinions.

Be aware of where people sit and their posture

As a general rule, people tend to *sit next to those they know and agree with*, especially if contentious issues might be raised in the meeting.

The astute chairperson will also note that people from the same department or section will not only sit near each other, they will also sit in the same way – their posture will be the same or very similar. This is referred to as *'posture congruence'*. Posture congruence indicates that the individuals *are at ease with each other* and may have *established rapport*.

It is also interesting to note that different groups of people may have different postures, so those from personnel may share the same posture as each other, those from engineering may share a different posture and so on. Posture congruence is an unconscious way of people recognising similarities and differences: *'we are different from them because we have a different posture from theirs.'*

Another aspect of posture is the *defensive posture* of those who may disagree with what is being said or who feel they or their department are being criticised. A common defensive posture is for the individual to sit *arms folded and ankles crossed*. Again, we must put this into context, as some individuals fold their arms when they are relaxing. A usual 'give-away' signal is when an individual's name or department is mentioned in a critical way and the individual actually folds their arms across their chest at that moment.

Figure 6.1: Posture congruence amongst Personnel and posture congruence for those in Accounts

There is often disagreement in meetings and this can be seen when a person looks at the speaker and *shakes their head slightly*. The chairperson should spot this and then ask that individual for their views, to bring out the issues.

Another subtle form of disagreement is when a member of the meeting starts picking imaginary pieces of fluff off their jacket. This, as we have mentioned before, is the 'picking lint' gesture.

Figure 6.2: Picking lint, silent disagreement

If disagreements between members become more overt, the chairman may see *finger-pointing* (*battoning*) in an accusatory way, people *moving their chairs back* or even *leaning forward* in an aggressive manner. Other overt gestures of disagreement can be seen in *desk thumping* with the *fist* and a *fist being used to punch the palm of the opposite hand*, as if in a mock punch to the other person.

We have even seen relatively silent members get so agitated about what is going on that they accidentally break pencils, usually with a loud snap.

If people in meetings decide to defend their views strongly or are unwilling to change then they might adopt the '*clamped shin cross*', where one leg rests with the ankle on the knee of the other leg whilst both hands clasp the shin of the resting leg. They are using both their legs and arms as a form of defensive barrier.

Figure 6.3: 'I am not going to change my mind'

Members who are listening intently to what is going on will show they are listening by *gazing at the speaker* or, in some cases, *holding their head up* or *tilting their head to one side*. This head-tilting is called the '*head cock*', a bit like a puppy taking interest in what is going on. In addition to the head cock, the listener may indicate agreement by a *slight nodding of the head* or even a non-verbal sound of agreement.

Next time you watch someone being interviewed on television look out for the sideways tilt of the head – it often seems to be exaggerated on television for some reason.

In some meetings an expert or consultant might be present and they may adopt the *high steepling* gesture, where the finger-tips of both hands touch but the palms do not, indicating a degree of confidence. If the steepling is at eye level, with the elbows on the table and the head tilting back, this can indicate a degree of smugness and superiority.

The successful chairperson of a meeting, by understanding body language, will be in control, will know the feelings of the members and will use his or her own body language to good effect. Meetings are about effective communications and so is body language.

Presentations

Presentations are given for the following reasons:

- To **inform**.
- To **justify**.
- To **instruct**.
- To **persuade**.
- To **sell**.
- To **entertain**.

It is clear that body language is of profound importance when giving a presentation because, as we mentioned in Chapter 1, as much as 90 per cent of face-to-face communication is non-verbal. So, to be a good presenter you need to be an expert in how to use body language when you are presenting and you also need to interpret the body language of the audience to be really effective.

It is interesting to note that the overt reasons for a presentation, for example, merely to *inform*, may hide the fact that the presenter might want to *sell* or *persuade*. It is these less obvious intentions of the presenter that come out in his or her body language.

The key point about presentation skills is that, with all the modern technology of presentation software, video and multi-media projectors, still the best and most outstanding audio visual aid is YOU!

Do not let modern technology get in the way of the best audio visual aid that has yet to be invented, the effective, live, human presenter.

Figure 6.4: The best audio visual aid is you

The body language of the presenter

In Chapter 1, we pointed out that we have developed body language expressions that express our emotions and feelings about events. If someone is said to be 'two-faced', it means they cannot be trusted because one part of them suggests one thing whilst the other, perhaps the body language, suggests the reverse. Needless to say, you do not trust someone who is 'two-faced'. The presenter must come over as sincere and trustworthy for the presentation to be successful.

An expression we use for an effective trustworthy presenter is that 'they had the audience in the palms of their hands'. This expression is derived from the fact that those who use the *double-handed upturned palms gesture* are more likely to be seen as *honest*, *open* and *sincere*. It is also no coincidence that ancient religious prophets are often depicted with two upturned, open palms.

When the *upturned palms* are associated with the *shrug of the shoulders*, this clearly indicates doubt, uncertainty or not knowing.

The gesture itself, as with all gestures, does not always convey that message, as it has to be put into context. If an individual is not

Figure 6.5: Mock honesty – 'Trust me – I'm in marketing'

trusted, for some reason, then the open palm gesture may be seen as devious. For example, if someone uttered 'Trust me – I'm in marketing' and used the open palm gesture, in an exaggerated manner, with the head tilted to one side in a rather pleading way, would you trust them?

One of the most important things about giving a presentation is to *make eye contact with the audience*. You, the presenter, have to give the impression you are addressing each member of the audience as an individual. This is where the overuse of audio visual aids can get in the way of effective presentations. The most obvious fault here is when the presenter chats away to the projector screen and loses contact with the audience.

Figure 6.6: The audience will pay less attention to you if you turn your back on them

The way to maintain eye contact with the audience is to *scan the audience in a random fashion*, resting your gaze on one person and then another. Do not start at the left hand corner and move round in a predictable fashion, this comes across as contrived; the unstructured random nature of your gaze will keep the audience looking at you.

Research shows that *presenters who maintain eye contact* with the audience are seen as being *persuasive, sincere, credible, honest, experienced and friendly*. As we saw in Chapter 1, the lack of eye contact is seen in a very negative way by most people. You are likely to be perceived as being out of your depth, uncertain, shy or having something to hide!

Most books on presentation skills warn against the presenter putting their hands in their pockets – generally a male habit. The reason for this is not that it looks slovenly and too 'laid-back' (to use another body language expression) but that *it prevents the presenter from utilising arm and hand movements to add emphasis*. Arm, hand and head movements should be used to emphasise key points.

As we have said above, the arms outstretched, palms up stance, is perceived as open, honest and sincere. It is also seen in other contexts as having a degree of doubt and uncertainty about some issue. Often, *the palms are turned up*, *the head tilts on one side* and *the eyebrows are raised*, usually followed rapidly with the words 'I don't know' or 'I've got no idea'. This may be a good response to a difficult question raised by an individual during question time at the end of the presentation.

We have mentioned the palms up gesture because the reverse gesture, *arms outstretched and palms down* actually means *assurance* and *certainty*. It is a good idea to use this gesture to convey solid facts or verified data. Again, we can see how body language adds weight to the words that we use.

It might be useful to mention *body language leakage* in the above context. If a presenter maintains that these are the 'facts' but uses the 'palms up' expression (meaning doubt) the audience may become confused: he or she is saying one thing but conveying the reverse message by the gesture. If the body language conveys one message (I am *uncertain*) but the words say another (here are the *facts*), then what will the audience believe? The answer is that the audience will, at best, be confused but most of the time *they will believe the body language* and therefore not trust the verbal message; the presenter is no longer trustworthy.

Another common leakage is when people say they 'agree' or say 'yes', but their head slightly shakes as if they really want to disagree or say 'No'. Again, those listening will subconsciously pick up the leaked message via the head shake and not believe the words.

We have suggested that the effective presenter will use body language to add emphasis to the message, but do not forget, body language also includes tone of voice, volume and pauses. The effective presenter will use the voice to project words to the audience and use the voice to add emphasis to the message. Another voice technique is to *repeat key words* in an assertive and enthusiastic manner. Although the good presenter may not want to sound like a market trader to get the point across, repetition can be very effective.

'The continuous improvement and lean thinking policies adopted in our department did not lead to a saving of £100,000 p.a., not even £200,000, but a saving of £400,000, straight off the bottom line – £400,000!'

The last '£400,000' was delivered with emphasis and with an effective pause for the audience to absorb the message. If the presenter had just said: 'Our department saved £400,000 by adopting continuous improvement and lean thinking techniques', the significance of the message may well have been lost on the audience.

Another key point is that successful presenters do not just state the facts, because facts seldom speak for themselves. The successful presenter uses the tone of voice and volume to show enthusiasm because *enthusiasm is infectious*, it is probably the only thing that people do not mind catching from others!

The effective presenter may actually use the *whole body* to add emphasis to the words they use. We are sure you have seen the dynamic presenter who bends his or her knees as if they are carrying a great weight. What they are saying is 'this is important, it has great weight, and I am offering it to you.' Often, the knee-bending goes along with the arms out in front as if they were carrying a heavy object of some kind.

Conducting your presentation – the power of hand gestures to make a point

Generally speaking, open hand gestures and even some forms of palms-up gestures indicate that the presenter wants to *establish rapport* with the audience. Depending on the context, these open hand gestures can range from indicating honesty, sincerity, openness or even begging and pleading. Again, we use the expression 'open-handed' to mean open and trustworthy.

Putting the *hands together as if in prayer* can add a degree of sincerity to the words 'we hope' or 'I hope'. The implication is that 'we hope and pray' or 'I hope and pray'. We are all aware of presenters who use the distance between their hands to indicate size, like a fisherman exaggerating a catch. The closer the hands are together, the smaller and more precise the message.

Using one hand where the *thumb and index finger nearly touch*, especially *near the face* is another way of indicating precision, small size or the delicacy of the information. If the thumb and index finger actually touch and this gesture is done near the lips then this conveys a different message, the message of exquisite taste, especially if this is associated with a kissing of the lips.

As with running meetings, the presenter should *avoid battoning* (pointing a finger) at individuals in the audience or the audience in general; as we have said before, this is seen as aggressive and rude. Another gesture to avoid is using the finger to *jab at the audience*; this is seen as adding to a verbal attack. Some presenters use a *raised finger in a beating motion* as if they were 'hammering home' a point. Again, the audience may feel they are being attacked. It depends on what impression the presenter wants to leave behind but they will not make many friends in the audience.

The only presenters who are likely to get away with this 'lecturing' style would be senior people in organisations who have recognised *coercive power* that is seen as legitimate.

It is interesting to note that those who give political presentations, or speeches, may *hammer home their emotional point* by using a *clenched fist* that they seem to brandish in front of them. Such gestures are used to encourage the audience to adopt *aggressive feelings* towards those they oppose. Many dictators are exponents of this aggressive style of presentation. The important point is that the clenched fist associated with aggression is used in the context of aggression directed at a common enemy; not the audience itself.

Behaviours to avoid

A final point is that some unconscious aspects of the presenter's body language can get in the way of an effective presentation. We have already mentioned the hands in the pockets as being restrictive. Also, the presenter who is rather *static* or *unanimated* is seen as cold and unfriendly, because being rooted to the spot certainly does not add to enthusiasm.

Losing eye contact with the audience, for example, by staring up at the ceiling, may lose the audience's attention; but *turning your back* on them and talking to the projector screen will really annoy them and may be seen as offensive.

Other errors that a presenter can make are: *frequently walking across the stage or into the audience*, *moving from foot-to-foot* in a rhythmic fashion, *fiddling* with pens and pointers etc.; all of which get in the way of communicating the message.

Another error, which is very common, is the constant repetition of a phrase such as 'OK' or 'You know what I mean' – such expressions can be very irritating. Audiences may start counting the repeated phrase and stop listening to the message.

Keeping an eye on the audience

The most obvious advantage of keeping your eyes on the audience is that you can assess whether or not they are *receiving* the message, *understanding* the message and *agreeing with* the message. All good presenters do this and they pick up the information from the facial expressions, head movements, postures and gestures that are exhibited before them. Let us look at some examples.

The clearest message that might come from an audience is *agreement* or *disagreement*. This can be seen in several different ways. There is the obvious *head-shaking* in disagreement and conversely the *nod* in agreement. Sometimes the disagreement is also indicated by a frown and agreement by a smile.

Another less obvious sign of possible disagreement, often linked to defensiveness, is the member of the audience (there might be more than one who does this) who *crosses their legs* and *folds their arms*, especially at the mention of some controversial issue. Be aware, however, that the front row of an audience, who feel exposed, often cross their legs and fold their arms as a form of subconscious protection. They may not necessarily disagree or feel defensive.

You might also find that some individuals might *lean their chin on the thumb of one hand* with the *index finger pointing up over their cheek*. This can mean a form of interested or critical appraisal, they might not have made up their minds but they are assessing the situation. You should treat these people with caution; you do not know whether they agree or disagree with what you are saying.

Figure 6.7: Critical appraisal

As in meetings, the presenter should look out for the person who silently disagrees, the 'lint-picker'. They are conveying the message: 'I disagree with you but can't be bothered to argue with you.'

We mentioned in our discussion on meetings that some individuals, usually those from the same departments or with the same views, will sit with the same posture (posture congruence). So you might find a row of people with a posture of disagreement and a row of people with a posture of agreement. The astute presenter might choose to involve those who agree or disagree to help resolve points of contention.

Signs of boredom

The last thing a presenter wants is to come across as boring. This can be particularly difficult if the presentation is after lunch at a conference, when even the most dynamic of presenters would find this 'graveyard slot' a challenge.

It is not difficult to identify a person or persons who are bored during a presentation and this does give the presenter a chance to rescue the situation. One rather devious method, if the members of the audience are known to the presenter, is for the presenter to mention in passing the name of the individual who looks as if they are about to fall asleep. This usually results in the person suddenly waking up, in case they might be asked a question.

Bored people in the audience might indicate this state of mind in the following manner:

- Looking around the room or even at the ceiling.
- Resting the head on a hand.
- Yawning.
- Leaning back with legs outstretched.
- The eyes might close and the individual adopts a slumped posture.
- Drumming the fingers on the arms of the chair – this can also mean impatience.
- Linking the fingers of each hand together and circling the thumbs.

If there are signs of people getting bored then the presenter could become more animated and raise the volume of their voice or could move on quickly to a more interesting topic.

Being distracted

The key task of the presenter is to get the message across but occasionally some members of the audience can be a distraction. The first distraction is the enthusiastic member of the audience, who responds positively to the presenter's every word, *nodding and smiling* and *clearly being supportive*. Although the presenter is looking for such support, there is a danger that the presenter will *just focus on the friendly individual* and forget the rest of the audience.

Another distraction is the person in the audience who *gazes intently* at the presenter. One of the authors many years ago was giving a presentation when an attractive female in the front row smiled at him and began to lick her lips repeatedly. Whether this was conscious or not, the result was nearly presentation sabotage. We will explore more about how males and females may be influenced by gender signals in Chapter 9 – How can body langugae help me understand office life?

Another distraction is the individual who asks questions constantly, forcing the presenter to focus the presentation on their needs only. The last thing a presenter wants is to give the presentation to just one person. If there is such an individual in the audience, the presenter should *not catch their gaze but deliberately move their gaze* onto others in the audience.

Without body language, the presentation would be boring and meaningless. The presenter would come across as flat and lifeless, the audience would soon lose interest. A presenter who does not use body language to add emphasis and feeling might as well give up and just hand out his or her written notes!

INSTANT TIP

In meetings and presentations they are watching your every move and you must be watching theirs!

07

How can body language help me in selling?

Selling involves the transfer of goods and services for payment. The salesperson is highly motivated to sell whilst the prospective customer, in sales terminology often referred to as the 'prospect', may need to be persuaded to buy. The effective salesperson is one who can sell a product or service to those 'prospects' who, initially, had little intention to buy. Selling is the art of persuasion and, as every salesperson knows, they have to sell themselves before they can ever think of selling the product or service.

The purpose of this chapter is to give you an understanding of body language that will help you to sell and, in addition, help you to understand some of the sales techniques employed by those in the profession. In effect, you do not have to be in sales to benefit from this section. From the salesperson's point of view, an understanding of body language will provide a competitive advantage over others in sales who do not have the knowledge and skill. If two people are selling the same product or service, the clinching factor may well be how they use and interpret body language in the sales situation!

Remember that in Chapter 2, on politics in the office, we used French and Ravens' classification of 'social power' (1960). Let us now apply this model to the sales situation.

Position power

We have suggested that people in organisations have power over others because of their position or title. People obey them, or are influenced by them, for no other reason than their position in the hierarchy of the organisation. If we apply this concept to those in sales, we can see that *the salesperson does not have a high degree of position power*. Sales people are trying to sell a product or service to a potential or prospective customer. The prospect can always refuse to see them, say 'No' and refuse to buy.

The only situation where the salesperson might have position power over the buyer is if the product or service is highly desired by the prospective customer and there is only one person or company they can buy from. An extreme example is the sole supplier, such as the local council or the only petrol station for miles.

The lack of position power for those in sales has meant that sales organisations have tended to *build up the title* of those who are selling. These days, sales representatives have been given high status titles to build up their image and gain respect from the prospect. Business cards will often present the sales representative as a 'Regional Sales Executive' or 'Account Director', and in some cases the term 'Consultant' is used.

Those selling hearing aids, and similar products and services, will often use the term 'consultant' partly because it reflects their role of giving advice, and partly to disguise the fact that they are actually in the selling business; above all the term 'consultant' implies a degree of professionalism and respect.

There is always a danger that those in sales do not recognise their relative lack of power or, on the other hand, overcompensate for their lack of position power by being too servile.

If the salesperson does not recognise their relative lack of power, they can offend, irritate or put off the prospective customer. Taking account of this indicates the salesperson's recognition of the other party's need to be respected. All this means is that the salesperson should not keep the buyer waiting and should not allow their body language to convey messages of *irritation*, *urgency*, *aggression*, *arrogance*, *subservience* or *insincerity*.

The salesperson needs to steer a path between being overconfident or arrogant, on one hand, and being too humble, on the other.

One way sales people manage this dilemma is to start off the sales conversation with a list of pleasantries, *which must come across as sincere*! Typical pleasantries include things like: 'Thank you for seeing me, I know you are very busy', or 'I expect you are busy so I will not take up too much of your time', or 'I am very pleased that you found the time to see me', or 'What a very pleasant office you have'. Any such pleasantries should be stated in an assertive manner, not in a grovelling tone.

It is an unwritten rule that buyers will expect the salesperson to provide these pleasantries as a way of recognising their different power positions.

A key thing about the sales situation is that the salesperson is often in the buyer's *territory*. Door-to-door salespeople, for example, are told to ring the doorbell but, when the householder appears, they should *step back*, because standing too close to the householder will *invade their personal space*, and the householder will feel threatened.

In a similar way, the salesperson *should not stand too upright* and tower above the buyer – this is especially threatening if buyer and salesperson are in close proximity. On the other hand, there is the danger that the subservient salesperson will lower their height so much that they come across as grovelling. One can imagine the Uriah Heep posture of the slightly bent back, head tilted to one side and the hands slowly rubbing together uttering the words: 'I am a very humble person, a mere sales rep, have pity on me.'

If a salesperson enters the office of a prospective buyer, they should look relaxed *but not as relaxed as the buyer*, again reflecting the relative power of the buyer and salesperson. An extreme example will illustrate this point: the buyer is relaxed and puts his (it tends to be a male posture) feet on the desk, leans back with hands clasped behind his head. If the salesperson did the same, then the buyer would be offended. Similarly, if the buyer adopts the posture of superiority, hands clasped behind the head with legs in the cross four position; the salesperson should not do the same.

In some books on sales techniques, the salesperson is told to *imitate the posture or gestures of the buyer as a way of establishing rapport*. It is the contention of this book that such imitation should be viewed with caution and many postures and gestures should not be imitated at all!

In particular, the salesperson should *avoid all postures of superiority*, as they do not have the position power that goes with it. Postures to avoid are:

- Standing too upright next to the customer.
- Standing with arms akimbo.
- Standing with hands in pockets with thumbs out or thumbs in pockets with hand out – gives the impression of being in control and aloof.
- Standing with one or both hands holding onto the lapel of the jacket, because it exudes too much confidence and expertise in front of the buyer. It is OK for a barrister or a doctor, but not for people in sales.
- Striding down the corridor with the buyer, head up and hands behind the back.
- Head tilted up, looking down the nose at the buyer.

- Invading the buyer's territory by placing a case or sales material on the buyer's desk. Even if it is a big desk, the salesperson should ask permission first.
- If the buyer and salesperson are sharing a table – neutral territory – then the table tends to divide itself territorially into two halves. This is typically what happens with a restaurant table. The salesperson should not subconsciously offend the buyer by moving his or her items over to the buyer's side of the table. It is worth seeing this at work with colleagues next time you are dining with them: if you move your glass or napkin over to their side of the table, they will feel uneasy and may in fact move your glass back over the dividing line.

Reward power

There are two types of reward that the salesperson can offer:

The first is the reward of the product or service that is being sold. The buyer will make a purchase because he or she has a need for the product or service and therefore it is rewarding to them. In addition to this, if the buyer believes they have paid a fair price for the product or, better still, purchased it at a reduced price, this will also be seen as a reward. In some cases, the salesperson will describe the product or service in a way that indicates that it will solve the buyer's problems. All sales people are trained to differentiate between the product's Features, Advantages and Benefits (FAB). The features are the technical details that usually only technically minded people are interested in; the advantages are all the advantages that the product or service has in general terms; the benefits are the advantages of the product to the particular buyer. So, a car may have many technical features, it may have a two-litre engine, side impact barriers, above-average acceleration, low fuel consumption and so on. The advantages include such things like accelerating out of difficult situations, you and your passengers will survive a crash and fuel cost will be low. The particular buyer may only be interested in the benefits to them – safety and fuel consumption, for example. Good sales people try to find out the benefits the buyer is seeking and sell on these benefits. In this case, the benefits are the 'rewards' the customer is looking for.

The second reward that the salesperson might use is the psychological reward the buyer might get from interacting with the salesperson. Some salespersons are so charming and personable that their presence creates a rewarding interaction. Also, if the buyer feels respected and important, then the interaction with the salesperson is also rewarding.

One of the ways to create a rewarding situation is for the salesperson to create a situation of rapport with the buyer, and this rapport is nearly always created by body language. You should be aware that many books on the skills of selling emphasise the salesperson should initially sell themselves – sell yourself first and then the product.

Reward power – establishing rapport

It is well known that if you give a small present to someone, however small, the person becomes slightly indebted to you as the present giver. We knew a manager once who would offer an unsuspecting colleague a mint and then ask them for a favour, which they found difficult to refuse. It got to the point where colleagues in the know would ask what favour he wanted before they took the mint.

The most prolific gift givers, in the UK at least, are medical representatives. Next time you visit your doctor see just how many items on his or her desk come from pharmaceutical companies, such as pens, pencils, pads and so on. It got so out of hand in the past that a limit has been put on the type of 'gifts' that pharmaceutical companies can give. Gone are the days when a purchase of vaccines meant they arrive packaged in a free medical fridge!

Many sales books suggest that, to establish rapport with the buyer, the salesperson should *mimic the postures or gestures of the buyer, as long as they are positive or friendly postures or gestures.* To frown at a frowning buyer or to out-posture their posture of superiority would certainly be career-limiting for the salesperson. *This copying of postures and gestures is often referred to as 'matching' and 'mirroring'.*

Figure 7.1: Posture congruence

As we have seen, to sit, or stand, in the same way as the person being spoken to is referred to as *'posture congruence'*, and it has been noted that people who are relaxed together tend to do this. Our suggestion in this book is that it is risky to mimic the other person's posture (mirroring), but there is no harm in adopting a similar posture (matching). The salesperson may realise that they and the prospective buyer have already adopted a similar posture; the salesperson should not be too conscious of this but just see it as a good sign that rapport has been established.

When people establish rapport they often have the same gestures and seem to mimic each other; this is referred to as '*interactional synchronising*'. Again, the sales books seem to suggest that the effective salesperson should interact in this copycat manner – *this suggestion should be treated with caution*. A good example of interactional synchronising is when you are dining with someone and you both reach for the glass of wine together, or both reach for the cup of coffee together. This is so common in restaurants that it is worth looking out for.

Should the salesperson deliberately synchronise their gestures with the potential buyer to help establish rapport? The answer to this is 'No'. The reason for this is that subtle body language messages, such as facial expressions and eye movements, have suggested that one of the parties is about to pick up their glass of wine. The other person picks up the subconscious message and the result is that they both reach out for their glass of wine *at exactly the same time*. Because the action or gesture happened at exactly the same time, this is not mimicking or copying. If the salesperson did try to mimic, they might be seen to be deliberately copying the other person a few seconds later and be seen as insincere. The salesperson can pick up the gesture but should do so with a respectful gap between the observation of the gesture and the follow-up gesture.

The key point about the psychological rewards the buyer is subconsciously looking for is that the buyer should come away from the interaction feeling respected, important and will have made up his or her own mind about the purchase. The words the salesperson uses are important but in face-to-face interaction, 90 per cent of the meanings, feelings and emotions are delivered nonverbally. Therefore, body language is of crucial importance to those in sales.

Coercive power

As we have suggested earlier, the salesperson is unlikely to have coercive power. Clearly, if the salesperson uses coercive techniques, not only would it be immoral but also the salesperson would never be able to sell to that customer again. The relevance of coercive power in the sales situation is that the buyer's position power may allow them to be abrupt, rude, aggressive and sarcastic to the salesperson. The salesperson may take the abuse and try to win the buyer round or politely remove themselves from the interaction. Never fight back; sales people never know when they might have to meet the buyer again.

If a salesperson is interacting with a buyer, the salesperson may feel uncomfortable, insecure or not respected. In such a situation, it may not be what the buyer is saying that is offending the salesperson; it is probably the buyer's body language and tone of voice.

The buyer's body language might consist of some of the following.

Postures of superiority
Arms akimbo, thumbs in pockets, looking down their nose or looking over the head of the salesperson at someone more important to talk to.

Gestures of impatience
Finger-drumming, sighing, eye-rolling and even looking away – for example, out of the window.

Gestures of disagreement
The most common one is the buyer shaking their head slightly as they listen. They have not said 'no' but it is an indication that they disagree or are yet to be convinced. If they nod slowly, this merely indicates they are listening and paying attention. If they nod rapidly, they are indicating they agree with what is being said.

Gestures of decision-making

If the buyer has made up their mind about the purchase of the product or service they may adopt the steepling gesture, with fingers touching, palms apart like a church steeple. If the buyer has made up their mind, then the salesperson should close the sales pitch and ask for the order or ask questions to ascertain objections.

Postures of resistance

David Lambert (1996) points out that when people are nervous or negative but want to suppress these feelings they sit with their ankles crossed and often with their arms folded. In some cases, the buyer might sit with 'one leg drawn up behind the other leg and pressed against its calf'. This is described as the foot lock. When in a standing position the foot lock can be seen with 'one leg drawn up so that its foot presses against the calf of the supporting leg'. A person might assume this position when resisting a sales proposition. The salesperson should look out for these negative messages.

Figure 7.2: 'You can carry on talking but I am resisting'

Tone of voice

By tone of voice, the buyer can indicate impatience and wanting the salesperson to finish the sales pitch quickly. The buyer may say: 'Tell me more,' or 'Really, do go on' or 'You don't say'. The tone of voice will indicate whether they really want the salesperson to give them more information or whether they have heard it all before and really want the salesperson to cease talking (this is usually delivered in a sarcastic tone).

How should the salesperson respond?

In the situation above, the salesperson should take note of the buyer's postures and gestures of superiority and subtly try to ingratiate him or herself with the buyer. The subtle use of flattery might help but the salesperson should never grovel or come across as subservient. Feed the buyer's ego, but in an assertive and not submissive way.

If the buyer is indicating that the salesperson should move on from the present sales pitch by tone of voice, or postures and gestures of impatience, the salesperson should rapidly finish what they are saying and sum up with a positive question such as, 'From what I have said so far, what are the features of our product/service that are of interest to you?' or 'Perhaps I have not convinced you about some aspects of the product/service. Where are your doubts?'

If the buyer is indicating resistance to the sales pitch, such as adopting the foot lock position, the salesperson could move on to asking questions such as: 'Let us review the main areas of your needs, what are you really looking for?' In this way, the salesperson is getting more information from the buyer and can emphasise the benefits to them.

Expert power

A fundamental question the salesperson should ask themselves is: 'Should I come across as an expert or not?' The answer to this question is dependent upon the expectations of the prospective customer. Basically, in some cases, the customer expects the salesperson to have expertise and to exhibit it, but in other cases, the customer wants to see themselves as the expert. Needless to say, no one is going to say: 'I am an expert, listen to me.' What they are going to do is inform the other party, by their body language, that they have expertise.

To illustrate this point, it would be unwise for a medical representative to assume medical expertise in front of a doctor or consultant, even if the medical representative does know more about the drug in question than the doctor does. In the case of a prospective customer visiting a solicitor or barrister, both professions are selling expertise, so their customers expect them to come across as experts. The last thing the client wants to hear is that their lawyer has doubts and is uncertain!

Again, the salesperson has to find out subtly whether or not the prospective customer wants to be seen as the expert or whether they expect the salesperson to be the expert – another dilemma for those in sales!

The astute salesperson can tell by the body language of the prospective customer if they want the salesperson to come across as an expert or not. Often this indication is subtle and it will be detected in the prospective customer's tone of voice.

In this example, the customer might look at the salesperson and say: 'Go on, tell me more.' By listening to the tone of voice this expression could mean:

1. 'I am interested please give me more information'; or

2. 'I'll humour him/her for the moment, but I am not convinced'; or

3. (If it is a sarcastic tone of voice) 'I don't want you to tell
   me more, I know it already'.

Salesperson as non-expert

If the salesperson has calculated that the prospective customer
needs to feel they are the expert, then the salesperson should be
assertive but not submissive. In addition, the salesperson should
come across as an understanding person who is willing to be
guided by the customer's requirements. Good questioning skills
are needed by the salesperson. The salesperson's body language
should be as follows:

- Slight stoop, not coming across as upright and aloof or
  dominant. The expression 'bowing to someone's
  expertise' is an indication that non-experts lower their
  height to those who have superior knowledge.
- Nods of the head, so as to give the customer the feeling
  that the salesperson is listening and agreeing – slow nods
  for listening and more rapid nods for agreement.
- When the salesperson is listening, the head might be
  tilted to one side – the head cock. This indicates listening
  and paying attention.
- The salesperson should use the palms-up gesture to
  indicate openness and sincerity.
- Not covering the mouth with a hand as if they do not
  believe what they are saying or what the customer is
  saying. As we saw before, people are apt to do this
  and/or touch their nose when they are hearing lies or
  telling lies. In this case, it may indicate a degree of
  uncertainty.

- Palms-down gesture, indicating certainty, could be used when agreeing with the prospective customer. Implication being 'Yes I agree, it is a fact.'
- Avoidance of all gestures and postures of superiority: arms akimbo, holding the lapel with thumbs up, walking with hands behind the back, thumbs in pockets, looking down the nose and so on.
- Make written notes of the key points that the customer is saying. These notes may or may not be necessary from the salesperson's point of view but the physical gesture of making notes gives the impression to the customer that their comments are important and so is the customer.

The impression the salesperson wants to give is that the customer is in control, the customer is making the decisions, the customer has the power and the customer is the expert. As the saying goes, 'it is not what you say it is the way that you say it!'

Salesperson as expert

As we have indicated, some sales situations require the salesperson to be the expert, especially if the customer is buying from a high-status professional and the sales situation is more like a consultation. In the customer's eyes, the potential purchase of a product or service depends on the salesperson coming across as an expert. The salesperson should appear confident, knowledgeable and in control. Usually in these situations, the potential customer visits the 'professional' person and is very likely to agree to the purchase of the service or the contract. Many professional people lose customers because they give the impression of doubt or uncertainty, when the customer needed assurance.

Let us assume a prospective client visits a solicitor to see if the solicitor can help them. Let us imagine that the solicitor listens intently but shakes their head occasionally and keeps using the palms up gesture with shrugs of the shoulders. The solicitor's tone of voice is also hesitant and he or she keeps using non-assertive words like, 'I hope', 'I am not certain' or, as one solicitor said to one of the authors once, 'Don't expect justice'. In addition, the so-called expert may look down at their feet and avoid eye contact with the potential client. All this may be honest and true but the prospective client does not want to hear the hesitant words and see hesitant body language.

The professional who will win the day and get more business is the professional who comes across as confident and expert. Such situations require the salesperson, in this case the professional expert, to adopt the following body language:

● Good confident eye contact with infrequent blinking.
● Upright stance with shoulders back – standing tall.
● Hand on the lapel with thumb out, or thumbs in pockets.
● Head up – very effective if wearing glasses. Indicates: 'I'm in control, I am superior to this situation and I am the expert.'
● Palms down in the gesture of certainty.
● Steepling of the hands, either on the desk or on the lap.
● If smoking, tilt the head back and blow the smoke upwards. (If they had negative feelings, they would tend to blow the smoke downwards.)
● Stand up arms akimbo, legs apart as if about to take action right now. The implication being: 'Leave it with me and I will solve your problem for you.'
● A strong handshake when meeting and parting, depending on cultural background of the customer.

Referent power

As we saw before, this refers to the personality of the individual, as seen by others: they are perceived as influential and powerful, they have charisma. Let us look at the situation where the salesperson has charisma and then where the buyer has charisma.

Charismatic salesperson

In this case, the salesperson has been attributed with the qualities of charisma and the potential customer has heard about their reputation or has met them previously. (Do not forget, it is the contention of this book that charisma is a social quality that resides largely in the 'eyes of the beholder'.)

It is clear in this case that the salesperson with charisma will have a huge advantage over others in sales who do not have this quality. Not only does the customer feel honoured to be in their presence, he or she is likely to buy merely because it is the charismatic person who is selling. It is as if Richard Branson or Alan Sugar themselves had sold you a product or service. In this case, the customers would probably pay extra when being sold to by such charismatic individuals.

It is important for the charismatic person to live up to their reputation. They should sell with a high degree of self-confidence and self-belief. It would be wise for the charismatic salesperson to treat the customer with personal respect and charm, so that the customer is honoured to be 'served' by such an individual. All the body language expressions of confidence, lack of doubt and charm can be employed. An appropriate handshake, a smile and showing respect for the customer would have them eating out of the charismatic salesperson's hand.

Charismatic customer

Here we have a problem for those in sales. The powerful image of the charismatic customer could cause the salesperson to adopt very subservient postures and gestures. It is often the stuff of comedy when a charismatic person is served by an ordinary mortal. Fawning or subservient behaviours are the order of the day and nearly always the result is a catastrophe. The charismatic person is annoyed and irritated and the sale is lost.

The answer is, of course, for the salesperson to remain calm and, above all, assertive.

Here is the approach to use:

- Maintain social distance between buyer and salesperson.
- Stand tall but less tall than the charismatic person.
- Avoid all aspects of body language that are seen as subservient, such as bowing too far, hand wringing, palms upright but too pleading, avoiding eye contact, too much nodding in agreement and so on.
- Avoid all body language expressions of superiority, as it will annoy the charismatic person.

Should the salesperson aim to be charismatic and develop referent power?

The answer to this is, 'No'. First, as we have said, others assign charisma to people; it is in the 'eyes of the beholder'. Having said that, the salesperson who develops their reward power and their expert power (expertise in selling and product knowledge) and acquires the verbal and non-verbal skills associated with all different sales situations may well gain the reputation for being charismatic.

Body language in telephone selling

If you look at some of your colleagues on the telephone, you will note two things about their body language. First, they do not stop their physical postures and gestures although the person on the end of the line cannot see them and, secondly, their tone and use of voice conveys the meaning, feelings and emotions.

Because posture and gesture are so bound up with verbal delivery, those trained in telephone selling are told to adopt the right posture when talking to prospective customers. In some cases, telesales people are told to stand upright, or even stand on the desk, so they sound dynamic and assertive. Those in telesales need to come across as friendly, confident, helpful and sincere. To do this they are taught the following:

- Stand with their head up, or at least sit upright with their head up. A slumped posture comes over in the voice, so it is to be avoided.
- Smile as they talk, so that the smile comes over in the voice.
- Reflect the other person's speed and tone of voice, as this helps to establish rapport. Most people do this anyway but in telesales there is the danger that the salesperson will get bored with the sales message and forget that it is another human being they are talking to, so they just sound like a robot to the potential customer. Needless to say, do not reflect the other person's tone of voice if they are angry, aggressive, abrupt or if they have a speech impediment.
- Another method of establishing rapport is to tune into the way of thinking of the person on the end of the line. As we saw in Chapter 1, there are three main ways people

think: *visual*, *auditory* and *kinaesthetic*. The way of thinking over the telephone can be identified by the words that people use, either *visual* words like 'see', 'picture', 'foggy' etc., or *auditory* words like 'sound', 'hear', 'loud' etc., or, finally, *kinaesthetic* words, such as 'touch', 'feel', 'texture', 'concrete' and so on. Getting on the same wavelength as the customer is important in the sales process. Although most people in sales do not deliberately estimate what mode of thinking the customer has, they usually adopt the same mode automatically. Perhaps the best advice is that those in sales should reflect back or mirror the words the customer is using.

The client's territory

When those in sales enter the client's territory, such as their firm or office, the salesperson is at a slight disadvantage. You may observe a salesperson, or any other visitor for that matter, entering the reception door and at the same time touch their cuff link or clasp their hands together or touch their watch. This gesture is subconscious and is a mild defence mechanism to do with entering the other person's territory.

If the salesperson has to wait in the reception area for the prospective customer to collect them, it is not wise for the sales them to sit down, especially on the low settees one often finds in reception areas. The reason for this is that when the customer does appear, they will be standing above and over the salesperson, putting them at a psychological disadvantage. In addition to this psychological disadvantage, when it comes to shaking hands, the customer is again at an advantage. To shake hands in an equal and assertive manner, both parties need to be standing.

The customer's office

The salesperson needs to accept the buyer's higher position power and the fact that the salesperson is entering into the buyer's territory. The following are useful tips:

● *Do not stand too upright* (lower your height slightly) *or too close* to the customer, as this is seen as too pushy or aggressive. Standing less than two feet (0.6 metre) from the customer invades their intimate space but more than nine feet is too impersonal. The correct distance is about *two to four feet* (0.6 to 1.2 metre). (In Arab cultures and with many people who live in hot climates, closer proximity is acceptable, so be aware of cultural differences – see Chapter 10.

● Be aware of posture congruence and interactional synchronising: *adopt similar body postures and gestures* but do not deliberately copy, as this will come across as contrived. Probably the best approach is to use *crossover mirroring*; in this case, the salesperson might imitate the buyer's hand-tapping with similar head-nodding.

● *Never adopt a more relaxed posture than the buyer* – remember the relative difference in position power.

● *The desk is the buyer's personal territory*, so the salesperson should ask for permission before putting documents and sales literature on the desk.

● The salesperson should use *active listening* techniques, such as the head cock or grunts/nods of agreement.

● *Maintain good eye contact* with the buyer, as this indicates confidence and sincerity.

● Remember that palms up indicate honesty, openness or doubt and palms down indicate facts and certainty.

● If the buyer places their thumb under their chin with their index finger pointing up over the chin, this indicates *critical evaluation* or that they are considering what the salesperson is saying. The buyer feels confident and has yet to make up their mind.

● If the buyer adopts the *steepling hand gesture*, then they have made up their mind about purchasing or not purchasing. The salesperson should close the sales pitch and ask for the order or ask what additional information the client needs to complete the sale.

We can conclude that effective salespeople are conscious or subconscious experts in body language and that is why they are so successful. Many an important sale has been won or lost merely by the body language messages people give and receive when they interact with each other.

INSTANT TIP

Establish rapport to make the potential buyer feel at ease and use body language to sell yourself – people buy from those they feel comfortable with.

08

How can body language help me in negotiations?

Negotiation is a life skill that everyone needs to learn in order to obtain the best value for themselves and their organisations. Many organisations have professional negotiators to obtain good sales deals and for negotiations between management and employee representatives. In work situations, everyone has to deal with other people, such as other employees, customers, suppliers, visitors and all the many other people who have a reason to interact with the organisation.

One of the key skills of negotiating is the ability to observe what is going on. We have already seen that body language comprises around 60 per cent of the meaning of a communication, so looking at the other party is essential to understanding. Observing enables you to check for the congruence of words and tone of voice with the accompanying body language. Where the body language does not support the works and/or the tone of voice, you should believe what you are seeing and not what you are hearing.

Whilst speaking is a conscious activity, body language is largely an unconscious activity. What we mean here, is that your *conscious mind* (mental processes that you are aware of and in control of) determines what to communicate and your *unconscious mind* (mental processes that are automatic and not under your conscious control) determines the body language element of the communication. This is why someone speaking truthfully shows congruent body language and why someone telling lies shows incongruent body language. As we have mentioned before, this form of body language, which does not support the verbal component of the message, is called 'leakage'. In other words, the real meaning is leaking out through the body language. Here are two examples that demonstrate leakage:

- A person who says, 'Yes, I will do that', accompanied by a 'sheepish' grin and lowering of the head, should not be believed.
- A person who says, 'We are experts in this technology', accompanied by a hand to face gesture, should not be believed.

Hand-to-face gestures provide a good indication that someone is not comfortable with what they are saying, indeed they may well be lying. These gestures include the mouth cover, nose touch, eye rub, ear touch, neck rub and collar pull.

Figure 8.1: The eye rub

Figure 8.2: The ear touch

Negotiating behaviour

We all need to influence people in our lives in order to achieve our aims, reduce resistance and resolve conflict.

When relating to other people our style of interaction will depend on the situation, the person/people we are trying to influence and the outcomes we are seeking. Our choices of behaviour will usually depend on how important the situation is to us, and will range from insisting on our needs being met, through willingness to consider the needs of others, to a 'couldn't care less' attitude.

These ways of behaving are represented in the Negotiating Behaviour Model, shown below:

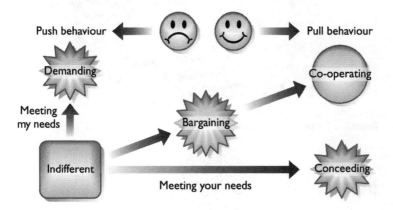

Figure 8.3: Negotiating Behaviour model

Demanding

Demanding behaviour involves a complete lack of consideration of the other party's needs. It can produce quick results in the short-term but usually causes resentment and often leads to hostility in the longer-term. Only use this style of behaviour when your needs are critical for you and/or when the relationship is short-term and unimportant to you.

Demanding body language in its extreme form involves an aggressive body posture, stern facial expression, harsh tone of voice with raised volume, prolonged eye contact and exaggerated gestures. Moving closer to invade the 'personal space' or standing over the victim of the behaviour may also be included.

Figure 8.4: Demanding body posture

Indifferent

Figure 8.5: Indifferent body posture

Indifferent behaviour involves a 'couldn't care less' attitude by one or more parties, usually because the issue does not affect them or is unimportant to them. Agreement is soon arrived at but the quality of the decision is usually poor for all concerned. Only use this style if you realise the outcome will cause no harm in any way.

Indifferent body language involves a 'laid-back' body posture, uninterested facial expression, normal or lowered voice volume, little eye contact and few, if any, gestures.

Conceding

Conceding behaviour involves allowing the other party to have their needs met at the expense of your own needs. Be aware that overuse of this behaviour will lead to others taking advantage of you, lowered self-esteem and frustration due to not having your needs met. Only use this style when maintaining the relationship is

Figure 8.6: Conceding body posture

more important than your needs or where you need to demonstrate compliance as part of your strategy to achieve your ultimate goal.

Conceding body language involves a normal or defensive body posture, apprehensive facial expression, low voice volume, poor eye contact and defensive or appeasing gestures.

Bargaining

Bargaining behaviour involves a willingness of all parties to appreciate the needs of others and to give up, usually reluctantly, some personal needs in order to have other needs met. The skill in bargaining is to give up needs that are less important to you in order to secure more important needs. Use this style when the goals of the parties involved are not complementary, such as in wage negotiations.

Bargaining body language involves the greatest range and flexibility in using body language to support your bargaining ploys:

- When things are important to you, use an assertive body posture, moderately serious facial expression, emphatic tone of voice, good eye contact and strong gestures.
- When you want to make the other party aware that their offer or response is inappropriate, use either:

  1. **Disgust** – through a rigid body posture, down-turned mouth, frowning eyes, head bowed, defensive crossed arms and eye contact either intense or avoided.

  2. **Derision** – through an open body posture, smirking face, upturned eyes and exaggerated gestures.

3. **Shock** – through a rigid body posture, open mouth, wide open eyes with raised eyebrows and an open, rigid arm gesture.

● When things are unimportant to you, a simple verbal affirmation and head nod will suffice.

Figure 8.7: Assertiveness

Figure 8.8: Disgust

Figure 8.9: Derision

Figure 8.10: Shock

Co-operating

Co-operating behaviour involves appreciating others' needs, working collaboratively together and a willingness to give up some personal needs in order to arrive at the most satisfactory outcome for all parties. The cost of using this style is in the additional time it takes for all parties to appreciate the needs of others and to agreeing the most positive outcome for all. Whenever you can, always try to use this style, as it leads to the most satisfactory outcome and to a positive long-term relationship.

Co-operating body language involves natural assertive body language for most of the time and using matching body language when you need to create or enhance rapport.

Push and pull behaviours

Whether you choose a *push or pull* style of behaviour will depend on how much you need compliance to how much you need co-operation.

Push behaviour

Push behaviour asks, requires, or demands that the other party complies with your bidding. It is usually delivered as a one-way communication, with the needs of the other party being largely disregarded. It is quick and effective when compliance is needed as a matter or urgency, such as when insisting people leave the building when the emergency alarm has sounded. It is less effective when willing co-operation is important, such as agreeing how people should work together.

Figure 8.11: Push behaviour

Push behaviour body language will involve an assertive body posture, serious facial expression, moderately raised voice, good eye contact and firm, directive hand gestures.

Pull behaviour

Pull behaviour describes, invites or sells to the other party ways forward that they are likely to find attractive, in order for them to comply willingly with outcomes that you are seeking. This behaviour involves a greater investment in time than '*push*' behaviour but the outcomes can be more satisfactory in the longer-term. Use it when it is best for the other party to select/find their own way forward. Do not use it when compliance to your requirements is essential or critical.

Pull behaviour body language will involve a relaxed and open body posture, friendly facial expression and tone of voice, and expressive gestures.

Figure 8.12: Pull behaviour

In practice, in a negotiation situation, you are likely to use a combination of *push* and *pull* behaviours. Use *push* when establishing essential criteria and use *pull* when a degree of choice is acceptable. For example, use *push* to gain acceptance of predetermined requirements and use *pull* when agreeing how the requirements can best be achieved.

Negotiation guidelines

All business negotiations will benefit from an effective process and guidelines that will enable the parties to come to agreement in the most effective and efficient way. The process and guidelines we recommend are described below, along with key aspects of body language that support the interactive elements of the process.

Prepare

This stage is all about gathering information for preparing your approach, strategy and tactics for the negotiation. It is essential for complex negotiations and especially where an 'offer' or 'bid' document has to be prepared as a precursor to face-to-face negotiations.

Do your background research on the other party. Be aware of your ideal outcome and the fallback position beyond which you will not give concessions. Discover what outcome the other party desires, their strengths and weaknesses and, if you can, establish their likely fallback position. Decide your strategy and tactics for the negotiation.

You may have an opportunity to meet with the other parties to the negotiation prior to commencing the formal stages of negotiation. This is your opportunity to establish rapport, to acquire information essential to the negotiation and to gain information that may give you an advantage. People generally prefer to do business with people they like, so do your best to create a favourable impression. This involves gaining an understanding of the people and using etiquette that is acceptable to them.

Refer to Chapter 10 for guidance on the body language aspects of protocol and etiquette when meeting people from different cultural backgrounds.

If you are able to meet with the other parties to the negotiation during the preparation stage, your aim will be to gather information that may be of use to you during the formal stages of the negotiation. To be effective in this stage you will need to use good listening skills, and 'matching' and 'mirroring' behaviour to show empathy and create rapport. Your negotiating behaviour should be *co-operative*, as the people you converse with will have needs of their own and you should show that one of your aims is to help them meet their needs.

Occasionally, you may have to use *conceding* behaviour if you feel it necessary to divulge information you would rather not. The use of *conceding* behaviour will be part of your strategy for establishing good relationships with the other party in order to achieve your overall aims. Decide beforehand what you can and cannot concede and be aware that offering a concession will often lead to the other party offering a concession also.

The body language you will use will be co-operative, respectful and friendly. *Demanding*, *bargaining* and *indifferent* behaviour is not appropriate in this stage.

Positioning

How do you want to start the negotiation? You may want to set out your parameters immediately, in order to give signals to the other party of your position or expectations for the negotiation. This approach may lead to a quicker negotiation or may lead to entrenched positions, if the other party finds your positioning completely unacceptable. Alternatively, start by finding out the other party's position. This has the advantage that you can start bargaining from where they are to where you want them to be. However, their opening position may be so far removed from what you expected that you realise your prepared tactics will not work and you find yourself at a disadvantage.

If you state your position first, be clear about where you will use *push* and *pull* behaviours. Use *push* behaviour by adopting an assertive body posture, serious facial expression, moderately raised and voice, good eye contact and firm hand gestures when proposing the essential aspects of your position. Use *pull* behaviour by adopting a relaxed body posture; a friendly facial expression and tone of voice; and expressive gestures when proposing the advantages, benefits and options for consideration.

Ask questions

Consider what questions you need to ask the other party in order to find out the information you need that will help you to decide the tactics you will use.

Start by asking *open* questions that open up the conversation, such as: 'What are you looking for?' 'What outcomes are you hoping to achieve in this meeting?', 'How can we meet your needs?', 'What are the most important things for you?'

Use *closed* questions that direct the conversation to specific areas, to find out what their main needs are. For example, ask: 'What are the most important things you are seeking?', 'What is not important to you?'.

Use *probe* questions that seek out more information, to find out the details you need. For example, say: 'Regarding the … *most important thing* … what makes it most important?', 'You say that delivery on time is essential, so what delivery dates do you need?', 'Please tell me more about ...?'.

When you ask questions to obtain information, adopt a body posture and tone of voice that matches the other party's to a reasonable degree, to help them feel relaxed. Make frequent short eye contact, observe their body language, looking for the degree of congruence with the words used, and show attentive listening with appropriate utterances and facial expressions.

When you ask questions to obtain compliance, adopt an assertive body posture, serious facial expression, moderately loud voice, minimal gestures and strong eye contact.

Listen

Only by *attentive* and active *listening* will you truly find out what the other party *needs* and *wants*. *Needs* are the things *essential* for agreement for a successful outcome. *Wants* are the elements that are not essential but the other party is seeking to include them in order to *enhance* the deal they get. These *wants*, are the elements they will be willing to trade for concessions from you.

When you listen, paraphrase back to the other party what you understand them to be saying. This affirms that you have listened and understood, and creates rapport. You will be corrected if your understanding does not match their intention. When paraphrasing, you may attempt to prioritise their demands and so shift their expectations. For example, say: 'I hear you saying that speed of delivery is essential to you and this has a higher priority than price. Is that correct?'

In the example, by adding the *qualifier* of 'Is that correct?' after the paraphrase, you are asking them to agree with you. Use this type of *agreement qualifier* frequently, because it confirms agreements and helps to keep you in control of the negotiation. It also creates what we call a '*yes set*' in the other party. To create a *yes set*, frequently ask the other party to confirm things you are confident they will agree with. Start with the easy and non-contentious issues where you know that agreement will be easy to obtain and then move on to the more contentious issues. Once you have created an *agreement mindset* in the other party, it becomes easier for them to continue to agree with you than to start challenging you. Of course, when using this technique you need to be very observant of the body language of the other party, so that you only add the *agreement qualifier* when their reaction to your statement is indicative of agreement. Sometimes you will need to pause after the statement to read their reaction before deciding whether the agreement qualifier is likely to be successful. Here are some other *agreement qualifiers* to try: 'Does that make sense?', 'Does that sound right for you?', 'Is that okay?'.

Analyse

Many a good deal is lost because the negotiator failed to analyse the other party's position adequately. Often the drive to get a deal gets in the way of getting a good deal. Do take 'time out' if you need it to consider what has been said, seek guidance if it will help and then return to the negotiation. In complex negotiations, after a session of bargaining, both parties will break off the negotiation for an agreed period to analyse, reflect and obtain guidance before resuming the negotiation. It is often difficult for the main negotiator to analyse adequately during the negotiation, so do use more than one person when negotiating important contracts. The support negotiators, who are removed from the actual negotiation, can see the bigger picture and can detect and analyse the body language of the other party more easily. Support negotiators provide analysis and advice to the main negotiator or may even join the negotiation, if they have the expert knowledge that is called for.

It is a good idea for the negotiators to agree body language signals between themselves, so that they are able to pass information secretly from one to the other. For example, when the other party in the negotiation makes a proposal, the main negotiator can turn to the support negotiator for a subtle signal as to whether the proposal is acceptable or not. Signals such as facial movements, hand or finger positions, or even holding a pen one way or another can be used.

Bargain

It is not a negotiation if you do not bargain. Bargaining involves 'testing' and 'trading'. Testing is what you do when you are trying to establish the other party's position or ascertaining if they are likely to agree to your proposition. For example, you might say: 'Is cost of delivery to be included in the price of the equipment?', 'If we agree to the price you are asking, will you pay in advance of delivery?'.

'If' is a magic word in negotiating. It commits you to nothing, yet it tests where and how far the other party is willing to move. It also helps you to make progress towards closing the deal. In place of 'if', you could also use 'suppose'. The form of the questioning goes as follows:

- 'If we were able to …, would you be willing to …?'
- 'Suppose we were …, would you …?'
- 'If you were able to …, then we might be able to …'

'If' can also be used to park an issue that is stopping the negotiation from making progress. Say: 'If we can put this issue to one side for the moment, we can see what we can agree on and then return to this issue later. Does that make sense?' (Notice the *agreement qualifier*.) The purpose of doing this is so that it gives time to consider how to deal with the difficult issue and also that, by agreeing the other issues, the difficult issue is less likely to kill the deal.

While you are in the bargaining phase, you are likely to use a full range of body language as you initiate and respond to bargaining ploys with the other party. When you make a proposal, use *push* or *pull* body language, as appropriate and then wait for the other party's response. If there is a long pause and you are tempted to speak again, you will most likely add a concession to you proposal. Having made the proposal, adopt an attentive body posture, with good eye contact and wait for the response.

Trade concessions

Unless you can walk away from a deal easily, never go into a negotiation with only '*needs*' on your list of criteria. Needs are 'must haves' and leave you no room to negotiate. Always have some '*wants*'. Wants are the things you can use to trade as concessions with the other party. Be willing to give up (trade) a want in return for securing a need. Say, 'We will be willing to give up … *concession* … if you will agree to … *need* …'

Never give away a concession without getting a concession in return, unless the concession clinches the deal.

The body language to use when trading concessions is the same as for bargaining except that you will be using *pull* behaviour and not *push* behaviour.

Close

The whole purpose of the negotiation is to close the deal and you must focus on achieving this goal. Know what *you* need and find out what the other party needs. Bargain and trade to move towards closure, summarise from time to time on what has been agreed and what still needs to be decided. Resist the temptation to go back to an issue that was agreed earlier, as this can undo other areas of bargaining that have been agreed. By summarising progress, you make the other party aware that you are moving towards agreement and agreement becomes easy and natural. As you are getting very near to closure, say something like: 'If we can now agree on ... *item* ... we will have finalised our agreement. Is that not so?' (Notice the *agreement qualifier*.)

During the closure phase, be aware of conceding a last-minute concession. Many negotiators will use this ploy when they have got you at the point of closure, to squeeze one last thing out of you for nothing in return. If you have got a great deal, even with this last-minute concession, then agree to it. If you are not happy, then use the word 'if' to trade what they are asking for, for something you want.

A good way to signal that you are nearing closure is to start to tidy away any paperwork that you have been using in the negotiation, look at your watch, summarise the concluding agreement or smile and say something like: 'Are we agreed then?', whilst offering a handshake.

Push and pull

Push and *pull* are styles of negotiating. Use *push* on your needs. You do this by stating why your needs are important or essential to you and that you require agreement to these elements. If you can support your demands with irrefutable reasons, such as compliance with laws, company policy, etc., the other party will feel compelled to accept your needs. For example: 'Our policy is that all contract workers must undertake an annual company medical. You will be able to comply with this won't you?'

Use *pull* to invite the other party to agree with you and to make progress. Sometimes this involves giving them something they are seeking that also moves you towards closure, or by making them aware that if we can agree on this point it will be a significant step towards agreement. For example: 'We offer an annual medical to all our contract workers. Is that something that would be of value to you?'

Flexibility

Negotiation is about give and take and finding novel ways out of situations that appear to be deadlocked. People who cannot respond to the needs and wants of others find it almost impossible to reach agreement in situations requiring understanding and compromise. To be successful in negotiations, you must be continually willing to seek solutions that move you towards your desired outcome and, sometimes, this means changing your mind and giving up a 'battle' to improve your chances of winning the 'war'.

Behavioural flexibility is a key essential for all good negotiators. Your behaviour – real or acted – provides signals that the other party cannot ignore if they need/want to find agreement with you. Use your behaviour to set the tone of the negotiation and to steer it to a satisfactory conclusion. The person who is able to display the most flexibility of behaviour will ultimately control the situation and get the best deals.

INSTANT TIP

The outcome of the negotiation is based on the tone you set and that tone is nearly always non-verbal. To be in control means to look the part.

09

How can body language help me understand office life?

Work personalities

The way we work is an expression of our personality and our interest in the type of work we do. Our personality is derived from the genes we inherited from our parents, our upbringing and our choices about how we live our lives. Our body language is an expression of our personality, so let us consider some basic personality types to help us understand the types of behaviour and body language likely to be expressed by different personalities.

In terms of *assertiveness*, people may be positioned on a scale ranging from *dominating* to *accommodating*. Dominant people tend to be extrovert, outgoing, expressive and entrepreneurial, whilst accommodating people tend to be introvert, helpful, careful and cautious.

In terms of *work orientation*, people may be positioned on a scale ranging from *people-focused* to *task-focused*. People focused individuals will be more concerned with the human relationship aspects of work, whilst task-focused people will be more concerned with the task aspects of the work. These dimensions lead to four typical personality types that we experience at work, as shown in the diagram Figure 9.1.

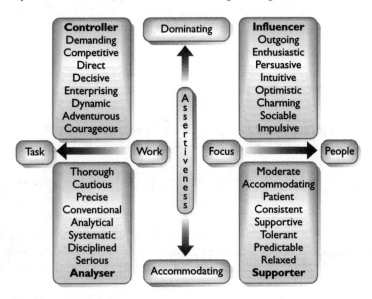

Figure 9.1: Personality types

Controller

Controllers tend to be forceful and direct, will tackle problems head-on and will assert their authority to ensure that others conform to their wishes. They are often enterprising, vigorous and ambitious, will bypass convention when it suits them, can come up with imaginative and unusual solutions, and will always try to do things in their own way. Controllers are the most likely to display aggressive body language. They will usually dress in smart, formal clothes in darker colours that emphasise their power and status.

When relating to controllers, focus on actions to achieve results and do not over-emphasise the human needs of the situation.

Difficult controllers are inclined to be domineering, stubborn, judgemental, aggressive and uncaring about the needs of others. To deal with difficult controllers, you must be assertive and sure of your facts relating to the situation being dealt with.

Influencer

Influencers tend to be individualistic, outgoing, people-orientated, persuasive and optimistic. They are generally warm and charming, and like to work with others in a constructive and harmonious atmosphere. They enjoy being the centre of attention, have social poise and usually make good hosts. Influencers are usually excellent communicators and are good at working with and motivating other people. However, because of their orientation towards people, they may be too trusting and unwilling to impose discipline. They are unlikely to be rigid in their opinions and will often compromise to reach workable solutions. They are usually quick at making decisions, relying more on intuition than hard factual analysis. Influencers will usually display friendly and assertive body language and are the most skilled in using communication and body language ploys to achieve their goals. They are likely to dress in the current fashion, often preferring brighter colours that get them noticed and that emphasise their individualism. When relating to influencers, focus on benefits rather than problems and avoid actions that may harm their egos.

Difficult influencers are inclined to be very self-centred, impulsive, undisciplined, manipulative, over optimistic and inattentive to the facts of the situation. To deal with difficult influencers, be friendly but assertive, be sure of your facts, be future-orientated and, most importantly, sell benefits that will appeal to their personality characteristics.

Supporter

Supporters tend to be friendly, easygoing, relaxed and undemonstrative. They work well as part of a team and like to build good relationships with their colleagues. In normal situations, they are contented and relaxed, have patience, will work steadily for sustained periods and may develop highly specialist skills. Supporters are willing and loyal workers, and because of this, it is easy to take advantage of them. They are usually reluctant to complain and, when a situation becomes intolerable, they are more inclined to seek a new situation than try to change the cause of the problem. Supporters will usually display very friendly body language and may find it difficult to use assertive behaviour, often agreeing when they do not agree for the sake of harmony. They will usually conform to the expected style of dress, preferring comfortable clothes in colours that allow them to blend in with others. When relating to supporters, be friendly, value their contributions and do not try to rush them into action too quickly.

Difficult supporters are inclined to be slow at responding to changing situations, are too compliant towards the needs of others and tend to avoid rather than confront conflict. To deal with difficult supporters, remain calm and friendly, emphasise how your proposals are for the good of everyone and ascertain how you can help the person to comply. With the supporter, you must be most vigilant in reading body language, because they will often say they agree for the sake of harmony when they do not actually agree; the real message will leak out in their body language signals.

Analyser

Analysers tend to be careful, cautious, controlled and systematic. They often approach situations more through their intellect than their emotions, which makes them good at work requiring careful thought, analysis and precision. They are usually hard-working, develop good task skills and are inclined to be perfectionist in the things they do. As they usually relate better to activities than to people, performing tasks working on their own is generally more enjoyable to them than the social requirements for team working. Through their thorough, careful and analytical approach, their decisions are soundly based but they may miss opportunities through being too thorough and cautious in their decision-making. Because of their cautious nature, analysers will often display defensive body language and will develop their own ways of working that are safe and secure for them. They will usually dress in a comfortable and efficient way for the work they do, and are unlikely to be interested in following fashion trends. When relating to analysers, be patient with their need for detail and their perfectionist orientation.

Difficult analysers are inclined to be averse to taking risks, obsessed with perfection, pessimistic and have difficulty in making and sustaining social relationships. To deal with difficult analysers, you must keep in mind their strengths and be willing to accept the negative side of their personality. When relating to them, try to give them the information and time they need but do remind them of the importance of deadlines. Generally, remain calm with them but on occasions it may be necessary to be very assertive if they start applying their own perfectionist standards to the detriment of specified requirements and deadlines.

Workspace

Everyone has some form of workspace at work that affords opportunities for expression of their needs and personality. The workspace may be an office or part of a general work area; a sales area; a locker, bag or briefcase for clothing, tools or paperwork; or even a vehicle if much of the time is spent travelling.

Most people will arrange and/or accessorise their work area as an expression of their needs and personality. What does your workspace say about you?

- **Controllers** – will typically organise their work area to be practical and effective. They are likely to accessorise it with useful objects and pictures or certificates that indicate achievement.
- **Influencers** – will typically make their work area a showcase of their outgoing personality. It may not be well organised but will be friendly, comfortable and possibly trendy. They are likely to accessorise the area with gadgets and novelty items, and may display pictures of their personal achievements.
- **Supporters** – will typically make their work area comfortable and friendly, although it may not be well organised. They are likely to accessorise it with pictures of family, friends and their work team; and may even include cuddly toys and amusing knick-knacks.
- **Analysers** – will typically make the work area an expression of their analytical and efficient personality. It will be well organised but not necessarily tidy and little consideration may be given to the comfort of visitors. They are likely to accessorise the area with functional items needed for their work and may see no reason to clutter the work area with pictures.

Territorial behaviour

Human beings, especially males, like most animals, are territorial. We need *personal space* around us so that we do not feel physically threatened – see Chapter 10 – and like to establish a territory within which we feel comfortable and in control. Do you feel comfortable in your work area by not having other people working in too close a proximity to you? Is your territory – the work area you operate in or control – large enough to satisfy your needs and/or your ego?

How is your territory delineated, so that you and others know it is your territory? What symbols or markers have you established that indicate it as your territory? For example, is it delineated by location, notices, entrances, colour scheme, layout, type of furniture or equipment etc.?

When working in your territory you are likely to feel comfortable, relaxed and in control. However, you will feel under threat when others attempt to interfere with or take over your territory. This usually happens through a reorganisation of work areas, change of organisational structure, altering reporting relationships, a new boss in charge of the area, or a predator who decides to acquire some or all of your territory.

To maintain your territory, you need to create positive relationships with people in higher authority who have the power to help you retain your territory. You also need to demonstrate your worth to the organisation, so that your bosses will not want to displease you.

If you come under threat from a predator, do not wait before acting, because once they have established a foothold, they will have a base from which to plan and operate their takeover. Make the individual aware, using assertive behaviour, that you will not tolerate their actions and also demand that your senior management back up your request to have the predator's actions curtailed or the person removed. This is a risky strategy, so you must be sure that the organisation values your contribution more than that of the predator. The alternative course of action is to remove yourself from the predator by seeking an alternative position and territory.

Ownership and status

Your territory is an indicator of what you 'own' in the organisation and the size of your territory may be an indicator of your status. When people come into your territory you are likely to feel more relaxed and in control than the visitor. Therefore, for important meetings, you should try to arrange them in your territory if you need to emphasise your control and status.

Ownership is often indicated by physical contact, such as opening a filing cabinet or putting your feet on a table or touching a colleague. You will have noticed in the press, pictures of celebrities in their grand homes, touching their expensive cars and even touching their partners to indicate ownership.

The reason for touching is that ownership confers power on the person in comparison with the other people who, by custom, are unable to act in this way. For example, if a visitor were to put their feet on your table, you would be affronted and would tell them immediately to desist in the behaviour. If you allow them to continue the behaviour, they will have established a degree of power in your territory and may continue to assume more control by placing their briefcase and paperwork on your desk. Soon you are in a subservient position and may find yourself even giving up your chair so that they can use your telephone. Be aware of these power ploys by visitors and do not allow yourself to be manipulated into loss of ownership, status and control.

Status is conferred on people by the positions they hold in the organisation and their ability to provide rewards and punishment. People who want to be successful with you, either will try to enhance your feelings of status to ingratiate themselves with you or will attempt to reduce your status to put them in a stronger position. An example of enhancing status is when a person may deliberately enhance your job title and importance to make you feel superior and then use this ploy to gain your agreement to a decision without referring to higher authority. An example of reducing status is when a person knows they are in a strong bargaining position and uses this knowledge to make you feel inferior to them, such as often happens when you call a service engineer to repair faulty equipment.

Table power

Most people in work attend meetings and these are often conducted whilst seated at a table. The type of table and where people sit can have an effect in terms of the power and influence established. So, let us look at the options for holding meetings around tables.

The first option is to have *no table* at all. People sit in chairs or stand at the meeting. This arrangement provides full access to reading body language and is particularly good for observing 'leakage'. However, many people feel uncomfortable and exposed without the protection of a 'table barrier' to sit behind and to arrange their paperwork on. If people feel uncomfortable without a table, they will display defensive body language and may not participate fully. Meetings without tables work well for short informal or impromptu meetings when the participants know one another well. They also work well when you want lots of interaction with people frequently forming different subgroups to consider issues.

The second option is to have a *round table*. Round tables facilitate open discussion, as there are no obvious 'power positions'. In addition, good eye contact can usually be established with everyone at the meeting.

The third option is to have a *square table*. As with round tables, there are no obvious power positions but where the most powerful person chooses to sit is likely to establish the power arrangement at the meeting. Eye contact is usually quite good in this arrangement and it facilitates open discussion. However, opposing factions are likely to sit opposite one another and this may lead to confrontational body language, such as aggressive eye contact, finger-pointing and fist-shaking.

The fourth option is to have a *rectangular table*. With a rectangular table, the main power positions are at the narrow ends and especially the end where a flip chart or projector is placed, as these items form a focus for attention. In addition, where the person controlling the meeting chooses to sit establishes power positions. If the controlling person is right-handed they tend to focus their attention more to their right-hand side than to their left-hand side, thus people sitting to their right are more likely to catch their attention and exert more influence. The converse applies if the controlling person is left-handed. As with square tables, opposing factions can sit opposite one another but you may forestall this by placing 'name cards' indicating where people are to sit.

When you attend meetings set up by other people, select a position that will give you the attention and power you need.

Greetings

You will be aware of the saying: '*You only get one chance to make a good first impression.*' Greetings are very important because they precede everything that follows and often set the tone of the relationship.

Greetings are especially important if you do business with people from other countries and other cultures, as the greetings protocol can vary widely. What is accepted in one country may be considered inappropriate in another country. Greetings are so important that we have devoted a great deal of attention to them in Chapter 10, where we discuss the protocol of greeting people from other countries and cultures.

In this section, we will consider the elements that make up the greeting and different forms of greetings that are used in most of Europe and North America.

Warning: do not apply the advice given below universally – read the advice on cultural aspects of greetings given in Chapter 10.

Greetings comprise *facial gestures*, *eye contact*, *body posture*, *handshake* and sometimes *other forms of touching*.

Facial expressions

Facial expression provides the best clue to the internal state of the other person. For example:

- A genuine smile indicates happiness and warmth.
- A false smile indicates underlying concerns.
- An expressionless face indicates a neutral position or it can mean the person is trying to cover up their true intentions.
- A strong grimace indicates an expectation of conflict.
- A slight grimace indicates concern and inferiority.

Eye contact

Eye contact during the greeting provides further clues about the attitude of the other person. For example:

- Good eye contact with smiling eyes indicates genuine pleasure in meeting the other person.
- Fleeting eye contact indicates concern and possibly inferiority.
- Sustained staring eye contact indicates superiority and perhaps an intention to intimidate.
- Avoiding eye contact indicates the person is completely uncomfortable with the situation and/or may have very low self-esteem or is trying to hide things.

- Looking over the person's shoulder indicates the desire to look for someone more important to talk to.
- Looking down your nose at the person indicates an attitude of superiority.

Body posture

Body posture provides a good indication of the status positioning of the person. For example:

- An open, slightly leaning forward posture indicates an intention of equal status.
- An upright formal posture indicates high status.
- A hunched up posture with a lowering of the head indicates an inferior status.

Handshake

Handshaking originated through showing the palms as a signal that the person was not carrying a weapon. Today, handshakes are an indication of welcome and trust when people meet and of thanks when they leave.

Handshakes can be quite complex, with a range of elements that provide clues to the status and intentions of the other person. For example:

- A strong grip indicates a need for high status, superiority and a resolute character.
- A firm grip indicates a moderately high status and an assertive orientation.
- A moderate grip indicates equal status and a friendly orientation.

- A light grip indicates feelings of lower status and a willingness to listen attentively.
- A weak grip indicates very low status and a willingness to comply to the other person's demands.

The position of the grip also provides clues to status and intentions. A grip offered with palm turned up slightly indicates willingness for openness and equal status. A grip offered with palm down indicates an intention of superiority, dominance and control. To disarm the intentional palm down control handshake, grasp the hand offered, step forward to invade the person's personal space to cause them alarm and at the same time twist their hand so that your palm is on top, step back and you now have the controlling hand position. A handshake of equality has both palms in a roughly vertical orientation.

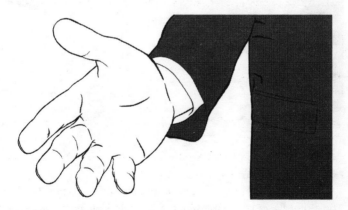

Figure 9.2: Openness offer handshake

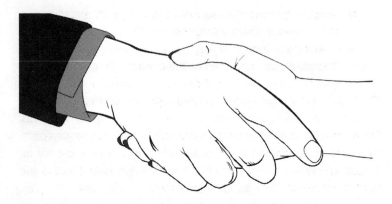

Figure 9.3: Dominant handshake – turns the other person's hand over so the hand and palm are on top of the other person's hand

Figure 9.4: Equality handshake

The duration of the handshake also indicates the attitude of the person. For example:

- Long duration (more than three seconds) with strong grip indicates an intention to dominate and control.
- Long duration with a light to moderate grip indicates an offer to be friendly.

- Medium duration (two to three seconds) with a light to firm grip indicates a willingness to follow normal protocol for handshaking.
- Short duration (less than two seconds) with any form of grip indicates the handshake as nothing more than a ritual to be got over with as quickly as possible.

The normal handshake includes the clasping of the other person's right hand. Handshakes can also include the left hand, usually to indicate greater degrees of warmth or control. For example, the left hand might be used in the following ways:

Double-handed
The left hand also clasps the other person's right hand to give a double-handed handshake as an expression of friendliness or affection. It also provides control on how long the handshake will last, because the other person's hand is completely enclosed. This handshake is usually resented unless you have already established a positive relationship with the other person.

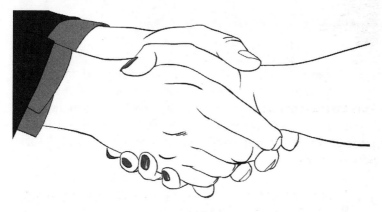

Figure 9.5 Double-handed handshake

Arm clasp

The left hand clasps the other person's right arm, anywhere from the wrist to the shoulder to indicate warmth and bonding between the two people. It also controls the right arm of the other person to a certain degree. The higher the clasp the more close and intimate the handshake will be. Again, avoid this handshake unless you are on very good terms with the other person.

Figure 9.6: Arm clasp handshake

Hug

The left hand extends over the person's shoulder and draws them into a hug to indicate affection or friendly relationship. It subjects the other person to direct body contact that may make them feel uncomfortable. This handshake is very intimate and usually has no place in a formal work setting.

Other forms of touching

The other forms of touching you may experience during greetings are as follows.

Handholding

In this greeting, both hands are extended out from the sides and lightly hold the other person's outstretched hands for the period of the verbal exchange. This greeting is open and friendly and usually only performed between women who are already well acquainted. Often the greeting will include compliments about the other person's appearance, which may be sincere or insincere.

Cheek-kissing

In this greeting, the hands lightly touch the other person's shoulders or sides and kisses are applied to one or both cheeks. Although the cheeks will usually touch, the kisses may not touch the cheeks. This greeting may be exchanged between females, or between males and females, but is not usually exchanged between two males in most of the Western world.

Body-hugging

In this greeting, both arms are clasped around the back of the other person, who is drawn in to close body contact. This greeting displays a great deal of warmth and affection and is usually reserved for family and very close friends. It generally has no place in formal work greetings.

Appearance

If other people were to look at you in your normal work clothes, would they be able to guess reasonably accurately the type of work you do and your status level?

Many jobs require people to wear some form of uniform, which are often symbols of what they do and may indicate their status. One of the authors was given a tour of a production facility and was asked to put on a white coat and protective glasses. During the tour, many disparaging comments were made towards the author. At the end of the tour, the author asked the guide for the reason for the unkind remarks and was told that he had unknowingly selected a supervisor's white coat to wear and this had upset the production employees.

A person's appearance comprises their gender, physique, bearing, clothes, accessories, grooming and body decoration. All of these factors may be changed to suit personal needs, to make an impact at work and to enhance career progress. Although gender appearance can be changed these days, we do not intend to discuss the topic further in this book.

Physique

Your physique is the height, shape and condition of your body. What does your physique say about you?

Research has shown that people who are taller than average are often considered to be more intelligent and more attractive. Desmond Morris, for example, found that male sales managers are on average taller than their sales staff. Unfortunately, if you are an adult and below average height, there is little you can do to change your physical height. However, you can select clothes that make you appear taller. The easiest way to add height is to wear shoes with taller heels. Women have an advantage here, because it is acceptable for them wear heels that can add about 4 inches (10 centimetres) in height, whereas men can only add about 2 inches (5 centimetres).

In terms of the shape and condition of your body, there are three classic body shapes, which are ectomorph, endomorph and mesomorph. People tend to perceive these different body shapes in the following ways.

Ectomorph
The ectomorph body is thin and fragile looking. Ectomorphs are usually considered intelligent, creative, self-conscious and introverted.

Endomorph
The endomorph body is soft and round with underdeveloped muscles. Endomorphs are usually considered sociable, tolerant, good-humoured and extrovert.

Mesomorph
The mesomorph body is hard and angular with well-developed muscles. Mesomorphs are usually considered courageous, action-orientated, competitive and insensitive to the needs of others.

Figure 9.7: Ectomorph, endomorph and mesomorph

If you find that your body shape is giving out signals about you that you do not like, consider changing your body shape through appropriate eating habits and exercise. However, do bear in mind that your genes will predispose you to a certain type of body, so you should not be over-optimistic about how much you can change your body shape.

Clothes

You will probably be aware of the old saying: *'clothes maketh the man.'* Whilst clothes cannot completely compensate for lack of knowledge, skills and application, they contribute a great deal to making a good first impression and to the way people react to you. What are your work clothes saying about you?

If you are required to wear a uniform or specific protective clothing at work, there is little you can do about this aspect of your appearance apart from making sure that the clothes you wear are maintained in as clean and smart a condition as possible.

Clothes contribute a great deal to your image. You will probably have noticed that when you wear good quality clothes you feel good, are more confident, have a better posture, speak with more conviction and other people pay more attention to you.

Wear clothes that suit your shape and enhance your image. If you want to appear:

- **Taller and thinner** – Wear darker colours, a single colour or very few colours, vertical stripes and tailored for a close fit.
- **Shorter and fatter** – Wear lighter colours, patterns with a mix of colours, horizontal stripes and tailored for a loose fit.

The colour of the clothes you wear will also have an effect on the way people react to you. Here is some guidance:

- **Black, charcoal grey and navy blue** can give you an air of authority.
- **Bright colours**, particularly reds, oranges, blues, greens and yellows, can make you appear, dynamic, confident and creative.
- **Dark colours**, particularly purples, blues, greens and browns, can make you appear calm, relaxed and caring.

- **Pastel shades** can make you appear gentle and with empathy.
- **White** can make you appear clean, fresh and pure.

Accessories

What accessories do you use to complement your clothes and to carry your essential belongings? We will consider footwear, jewellery and bags.

Footwear

Do you wear footwear that is comfortable, fashionable or essential for the type of work you do? What do your shoes say about you? Are they comfortable, smart, fashionable, practical, clean or dirty?

Shoes are often overlooked when it comes to dressing for work and yet many people will look straight at your shoes to assess the sort of person you are. For work, in order of priority, your shoes should be practical, comfortable, clean, smart and, lastly, fashionable. Of course, there will be occasions when exactly the reverse priority will apply, such as when it is important to impress someone and you select shoes to impress and to help you feel more confident.

Jewellery

Items of jewellery are personal adornments that allow you to express your personality and sometimes to express your wealth and status. It is normally more acceptable for females to wear jewellery than it is for males. In most work situations, jewellery should be kept to a minimum, selected to complement the clothes worn and should be of at least reasonable quality.

Jewellery should never be worn that might cause an accident or personal injury in the type of work you do. Most employees in manufacturing plants are not allowed to wear watches, rings, ties or any jewellery that could get caught in machinery.

Bags

Male-orientated clothes usually have plenty of pockets to carry essential personal belongings. Female-orientated clothes are much less likely to have adequate pockets for essential personal items, so women usually have to carry a handbag. The type of handbag used can say a lot about a woman. For some women it is large, containing every conceivable item that might be needed in a wide range of emergencies, whilst for others it is a small, fashionable container holding essential items only. Some men also carry handbags, but it is generally more acceptable for them to use a briefcase.

Both men and women often need to use a briefcase for their business paperwork or a portable computer holdall. Whatever type of bag you use to support you in your work, in order of priority it should be functional, in good condition and of smart appearance. As with shoes, however, sometimes the reverse priority will apply.

Grooming

Even more than with clothes, personal grooming speaks volumes about the sort of person you are. Grooming is mainly evident through personal cleanliness, hair, nails and, for women, make-up. What does your personal grooming say about you?

Cleanliness involves regular washing, teeth cleaning and paying particular attention to the cleanliness and condition of the skin, fingernails and toenails. Deodorant should be used as necessary, and aftershave and perfume used that is pleasant but not strongly scented.

Hair should be well cut in an appropriate style for the type of work and hair dye, in an appropriate colour, should be used if it enhances appearance. Men with beards and/or moustaches should keep them trimmed and of a style that suits their facial features. Both men and women should also consider removing excessive or unsightly hair to enhance appearance.

Women often wear make-up to enhance their appearance and they should ensure that the effect created by the make-up is appropriate and acceptable for the type of work they do.

Body decoration

Many people decorate their bodies with tattoos and with body piercing. Whilst this is usually acceptable in moderation, many people are offended by what they consider excessive body decoration. The point to make here is that if people are unable to see past the body decoration to the qualities of the person, then the body decoration is having a detrimental effect on the person's image and credibility.

Gender signals

Gender signals are the signals that give us clues about the masculinity or femininity of people. We all know that some men display very feminine traits and some women display very masculine traits. Whilst gender may be considered in 'black and white' terms, masculine and feminine behaviour has many shades of grey.

It is obvious that men and women have physical differences related to their roles in procreation. We should also realise that, through evolution, male and female brains are structured differently. The female brain has more connections between the left and right sides of the brain, which makes them better at multitasking. Through evolution, women are traditionally good at communicating, understanding body language, nurturing and caring, and men are good at providing, protecting and maintaining.

In most countries and cultures, men and women work alongside one another and this can sometimes cause difficulties due to their gender differences and especially when the social side of work leads to flirting and courtship displays. Everyone needs to feel valued and appreciated and this often leads to behaviour designed to attract attention and to receive compliments.

It is interesting to note that male and female employees who are a similar age, and therefore eligible as potential partners, will often joke with each other about that potentiality. Comments such as: 'I see you were out on the town last night', said with a knowing smile or 'You look smart … must be a new man/woman in your life', again said with a sideways smile, or cheeky smile. These rather knowing comments, said in a humorous, way may not be 'politically correct' but it is common banter in shop floor and office life. Such comments and body language are referred to as 'joking relationships' and subtly ease the sexual tension between those who work together.

Let us now explore some of the main gender signals males and females use to indicate their intentions in obvious, subtle and subliminal ways.

Male signals

Historically, males are hunters and usually take the initiative in signalling their intentions towards women and warnings towards men. Here are some of the typical male postures and their meanings.

Gazing
When a male likes a female, he will initially indicate his interest through *gaze* signals. He will allow his gaze to wander up and

down the woman's body and will occasionally try to make eye contact. If she is interested in him, she will return his eye contact. He will continue to gaze at her body and will extend the periods of eye contact, which will eventually lead to a smile, which, if returned, confirms she is willing for him to make an advance.

Preening
Animals preen to keep in good condition and to demonstrate to potential mates that they are a prime specimen. Males perform preening displays to women by adjusting their clothes and by combing or smoothing their hair. Some males use a subtle form of preening to find out if a woman is interested in them. This involves wearing their tie loose or to one side or placing a foreign object on their clothing, such as a piece of fluff, or being dishevelled in some other way. If the woman is interested in him, she will show her intentions with a pretext of correcting his appearance.

Stand tall posture
Men know that females prefer tall, fit men, so when a man wants to catch a woman's eye he will stand tall, holding in his stomach and filling his chest with air.

Cowboy posture
This position indicates 'I am a fit dude'. It involves hooking the thumbs into the top of their trousers with fingers pointing downwards, standing with one leg slightly bent with the foot pointing at the woman of interest and with the head slightly cocked in her direction.

Relaxed posture
This position indicates: 'I am relaxed and someone you can rely on.' It involves standing in a casual manner, with one hand in trouser, jacket or coat pocket and head lowered slightly. In a seated position, one ankle is placed on the knee of the other leg, with the hands holding the raised leg.

Figure 9.8: Cowboy posture

Aggressive posture
This position indicates: 'I am a tough guy.' It involves standing with feet shoulder width apart, hands on hips, trunk tilted slightly forward and direct, prolonged eye contact. This display is used to ward off other males and displayed to a female when the male thinks she is seeking a dominant male.

Superior posture
This position indicates: 'I am a smooth operator.' It involves sitting with legs outstretched and ankles crossed or with one ankle placed on the knee of the other leg and with both hands clasped behind the head. If possible, the chair is tilted back also. Another version of this posture when a table is nearby, is to place the feet on the table with the ankles crossed.

Casual posture
This position indicates: 'I am an easygoing sort of person.' It involves standing in a casual manner with one ankle crossed in front of the other, leaning with the shoulder against a wall and with arms folded or in trouser pockets. Variants of this posture include

placing a hand on the side of the head with the elbow touching the wall or the arm extended with the hand touching the wall.

Figure 9.9: Casual posture

Crotch posture

This position indicates: 'I am available.' It involves sitting down with the legs splayed apart offering a good view of the crotch.

Figure 9.10: Crotch posture – 'I am available'

Female signals

Historically, females are carers and nurturers who are protected by males. Females normally expect males to take the lead in overt signalling but they have many more subtle ways than men do of conveying their own signals to men and to women. Here are some of the typical female postures and their meanings.

Head-tilting
A woman will often tilt her head to one side at a man who interests her as a signal that she is interested and may be approached.

Figure 9.11: 'I am interested'

Gazing
When a female likes a male, she will provide fleeting gaze signals to indicate her interest. Usually, the head is tilted down slightly so that the eyes open wider when she gazes and then she will lower her eyes and look away. Often she will turn away slightly so that the gaze is given with head turned looking over her shoulder. If she becomes more interested, she will face the man, provide a direct gaze and may give a slight smile. A further indication of interest is a slightly open mouth and possibly a licking of the lips. When a

close proximity is established between two people, noticing a widening of the pupils is a confirming sign of interest.

Figure 9.12: The gaze of shy interest

Blushing
Many women will blush when they notice a man's interest in them. This may be a reciprocal sign of interest or it may be because the woman is embarrassed by the attention. Other body language signals should be looked for to confirm the cause of blushing.

Smoke signals
When a woman who is smoking converses with a man, she will exhale her cigarette smoke in an upward direction if she is interested in the man and in a downward direction if she has no interest in him. Smoke signals also indicate positive and negative feelings in both sexes. Smoke exhaled upwards indicates positive feelings and smoke exhaled downwards indicates negative feelings.

Figure 9.13: Positive smoke signals

Shoulder-lifting

Lifting one or both shoulders is a submissive signal and indicates that the woman will accept an approach from the man. Men may reciprocate this signal to show a non-threatening intention.

Preening

Women often use preening to direct the man's attention. She may take out her make-up mirror to check her lips and make-up, or even apply lipstick to direct his gaze to her mouth. She may look at her legs or adjust her hosiery to direct attention to her legs. She may even adjust her clothing around her bosom to direct his attention to her breasts.

Stroking

Similar to preening, a woman will often stroke parts of her anatomy that she wants to direct the man's attention to, such as stroking her hair, face, arms, abdomen, legs, feet etc. Similarly, she may fiddle with an earring, necklace, bracelet, buttons etc. She may also stroke or fiddle with objects that have a phallic connotation.

Aggressive posture

This position is similar to the male aggressive posture, except that the legs are kept closer together and one leg may be bent slightly forwards. The display is used to ward off inappropriate attention from males and as a warning signal to females.

Figure 9.14: Aggressive posture

Leg signals

When seated, a woman may hold her legs close together to accentuate the shape of her legs and will point her knees in the direction of her interest. When wearing a skirt or dress, a woman may cross her legs above the knee to expose her thigh to the man's gaze. She may also cross and uncross her legs slowly a number of times to draw the man's attention to her legs.

Figure 9.15: Leg signal

Foot signals

As with men, a woman will point one or both feet towards a man she is interested in and away from a man she has no interest in. She may also slip one foot partially out of her shoe or repeatedly move it in and out of her shoe as a sexual innuendo.

Bag signals

When a woman is not interested in a man who is making advances towards her, she may hold her bag as a barrier between herself and the man. If she is interested, the bag will be moved away, allowing for a more intimate contact.

Figure 9.16: Bag signal – 'I am not interested'

Summary

In this chapter, we have given you an insight to the world of working with colleagues that applies particularly in office settings but equally applies to other work settings.

You should now have an understanding of why people work and of what you most want from your life at work.

The exploration of the four different personality types will have made you aware of why people behave as they do and provided clues to their needs, behaviour and the types of work they enjoy.

You will now be aware of how to maintain or increase your ownership and status in your work setting and how to use tables at meetings to achieve your aims more easily.

Work relationships commence with greetings and you are now aware of the components that make up a greeting, the types of greetings to use and those to avoid.

Your appearance has a great impact on how people perceive you and often on the progress you make in your career. We hope the guidance provided on this topic will help you to present an appearance that enhances your success at work.

Finally, because many people like to create social relationships, flirt or seek out partners at work, you will now be aware of some of the main body language signals that males and females use to indicate their intentions and interest in others.

The chapters in this book provide guidance on the many other types of body language signals and their uses in specific work related contexts.

INSTANT TIP

Observe and understand and you will not be the last person to be aware of what is going on!

10

How can body language help me work with people from different cultures?

What do you need to know to work with people from other cultural backgrounds and to be successful in international business ventures?

The major continents of the world, their countries and the countries' regions all have their own cultural differences. This is due to the topography of the land and its climate; the historical colonisation of the land by people; and the national, religious and other cultural factors that influence traditions and customs.

Cultural diversity

Today, global integration and the ease of international travel is allowing people to move to countries that have different cultures, and, as they live, work and integrate into the new societies, they create a diverse cultural richness. This movement of people brings benefits to the communities but may also bring problems when their cultures clash.

To do business with other countries and cultures, you need to understand the basics of their cultural etiquette. Even people who do not conduct business in other countries, are working in increasingly diverse multicultural environments, where an understanding of the rudiments of accepted behaviour will be of value to establish rapport, manage and lead people.

Protocol

To be successful in working with people from other cultures, you need to understand the essentials of their social cultural norms, so as not to offend them through poor etiquette, including the inappropriate use of non-verbal gestures. When greeting and relating to people from other regions of the world and other cultures, the important cultural aspects of etiquette are termed 'protocol' and set the behaviour that is expected if a positive relationship is to be established.

Before visiting a foreign country to do business or when receiving foreign visitors, do some background research on the protocol to be used. You can purchase books that provide information and sources of information for country-by-country briefings on key aspects of the history, culture, etiquette and business practices (such as: *Kiss, Bow or Shake Hands* by Morrison and Conway (2006) and *Cultural Intelligence* by Thomas and Inkson (2003)), or you can find similar information using the internet. The key body language aspects of protocol to take into account are greetings, dress, proximity and gestures.

Greetings

The purpose of a greeting is to recognise the other person and to introduce yourself by giving your name and, where relevant, your job title and organisation. This may be followed with your reason for greeting the person, such as to act as an interpreter, guide, host, sales person, negotiator etc. The adage, that '*you never get a second chance to make a good first impression*' is particularly true for your first greeting to another person. The greeting often sets the tone and expectation on both sides for the relationship that is to follow. Normally, we want our greeting to be the first step in creating rapport with the other person so that we may be influential with them.

Dress

As an initial indicator of sameness or difference, dress either sets us apart when style and quality are very different or brings us closer together when style and quality are similar. Even before any greeting or words are exchanged, our dress is speaking volumes about who we are, what we stand for and our pretensions of or actual status. To work effectively with other people, you should try to emulate similarities in dress to help you establish rapport and co-operation. This does not mean copying national styles of dress when working with people from different world regions but it does mean emulating the formality or informality that their dress code is indicating. Sometimes we want dress to set us apart, as in the different modes of dress between the sexes, and when we want our dress to indicate status or role or to help us to be more influential.

Proximity

This relates to the distance you maintain between yourself and the other person, especially during the greeting. In many informal cultures and especially in warmer countries, such as southern Europe, Latin America and parts of Africa, the greeting will be informal, with close proximity, and may even include a prolonged body hug or handshake. In formal cultures and in many colder countries, the greeting will be formal, with distance between the bodies and touching or handshaking kept to a minimum.

Always bear in mind that people will feel uncomfortable and possibly intimidated if you sit or stand too close to them. Similarly, they may find you cold and aloof if you maintain too much distance. The amount of personal space needed is derived from personal preferences and cultural norms. Unless you know otherwise, it is better to keep a respectful distance until you observe what is comfortable for the other person. If you notice that the other person's colleagues maintain a close distance, this does not mean that it is acceptable for you to follow their lead. Allow the other person to dictate the acceptable amount of social distance as the relationship develops.

Proximity may be considered in terms of the amount of *personal space* we like around us at any given time. The personal space we need will vary according to our personality, cultural upbringing and to the situation. With friends, we will usually have no problem with close proximity and possibly even touching, but in most other situations we need more personal space until we become comfortable and relaxed.

There are three zones of personal space to consider. For people who live in more reserved cultures, these zones are:

● **Public zone** – around 4 to 6 feet (1.2 to 1.8 metres) when we are in situations where we do not know the other people.

● **Social zone** – around 2 to 4 feet (0.6 to 1.2 metres) in situations where we are on good terms with the other people.
● **Intimate zone** – less than 2 feet (0.6 metres) is reserved for people with whom we have a close relationship.

Figure 10.1: Personal space zones

For people in less reserved cultures, the above distances may be halved.

Getting closer to someone than they feel comfortable with will break rapport and may be interpreted as threatening behaviour, requiring a defensive response. Of course, the situation will have a bearing on the personal space we demand. People who live and work in urban areas will usually require less personal space than people who live and work in rural areas. Also, in crowded commuter situations and at large public gatherings a smaller amount of personal space will usually be tolerated.

Is touching acceptable? As a general guide, apart from the brief greeting ritual, it is advisable to avoid touching, especially members of the opposite sex.

Gestures

All effective communication includes gestures using the face, hands and body that support the verbal messages being communicated, and in some cases provide the whole message. Facial gestures are fairly universal and have similar meaning in most parts of the world, especially expressions related to joy, fear and anger. Other gestures, especially those involving the hands, can have very different meanings in different cultures, so you are advised to avoid hand gestures until you have ascertained their meaning in the cultural context they will be used. For example, forming an 'O' with the thumb and forefinger means 'OK' (okay) in much of the world, but can also mean zero, money, worthless, homosexual, or be a rude insult, depending on the regional and cultural context in which it is used.

Figure 10.2: This 'O' gesture means different things in different societies

In the next section, we will use this common 'OK' gesture as an example to show how gestures can have very different meanings in different parts of the world.

International protocol

In this book, we do not have the space to provide a complete coverage of body language protocol in all the countries of the world.

We will, however, endeavour to provide guidance on some of the key aspects of body language etiquette you need to pay attention to when interacting with people from other countries and cultures. We shall consider this in relation to the main continents and cultural areas of the world, shown on the world map in Figure 10.3.

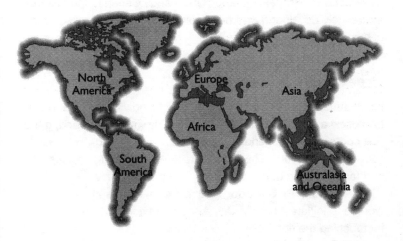

Figure 10.3: World regions

We will take each world area in turn and make you aware of the similarities and differences in terms of the protocol for initial business greetings, dress, proximity and gestures for the larger and/or more significant trading countries in the area. In most cultures, greetings may become more informal, friendly and close as the relationship develops.

We stress that the guidance given is for *business situations*, because some aspects of greetings, dress and proximity are likely to be different in a less formal, non-business context.

North America

North America is made up of the United States of America (USA), Canada, Mexico, the countries south of Mexico that border on South America and the countries that make up the Caribbean Islands. In terms of trade, North America includes the well-developed countries of the USA and Canada, and some moderately developed and developing countries in the south and in the Caribbean Islands.

Greetings

North Americans are largely open and friendly people. They will exchange a short-firm handshake, possibly with a head nod, good eye contact, and a friendly greeting, such as saying, 'Hi', 'Hello', 'Good to meet you'. The verbal greeting will usually include title and family name but expect soon to be on first name terms.

In **Canada, El Salvador** and **Mexico** men should wait for women to initiate a handshake. Also, in **Mexico** women may greet by touching the right forearm or shoulder.

In **El Salvador**, the handshake is gentle and may last more that a few seconds. The verbal exchange of title and family name should be in a soft tone, as loudness is disliked. Sometimes a nod is given in place of a handshake.

In **Guatemala**, people are softly spoken, will give a gentle handshake and may utter the greeting, 'Mucho gusto'.

Dress

For most of the region there are no special rules to follow regarding business dress, as casual dress is accepted in much of the business world, but some organisations have a more formal dress code for work. We advise you to check on dress code before you visit.

In **Canada, Mexico** and the southern countries, business dress is more formal and jeans are best avoided.

Proximity

As North Americans are generally open, friendly and often gregarious people, they do not need a large personal space; indeed, if you maintain too much space you may be regarded as aloof or as regarding yourself superior in some way.

In **Mexico** and countries in the south, personal space is usually much smaller than in other parts of the region and touching is usually acceptable. Maintaining too much distance is likely to be interpreted as unfriendly.

Gestures

North Americans may be moderately expressive with their hand gestures when talking and when making non-verbal signals and, due to the North American film and television industry, most people have become accustomed to the most typical gestures North Americans use.

In **Canada**, maintain friendly but reserved behaviour and follow good rules of etiquette. If you tend to use expansive arm gestures when talking, restrain yourself when talking with Canadians – except with French Canadians who speak in a more demonstrative fashion.

In **Costa Rica** and **Guatemala,** making a fist with the thumb sticking out between the middle and index fingers is obscene. In **Guatemala**, the 'OK' gesture is also obscene.

In **El Salvador**, although people are expressive with their hands, it is rude to point your finger at another person. Yawning in public should be avoided.

Mexicans may not make eye contact. This is a sign of respect and should not be interpreted as evasiveness or low self-esteem. Mexican men are generally open and friendly, and make a lot of physical contact. Touching shoulders or holding another's arm is common and to withdraw from this touch may be taken as an insult. Mexicans use a 'psst-psst' sound to gain another's attention in public, so do not be affronted if it is used on you.

In the **USA**, the 'OK' gesture means 'okay'. Do not use an upward pointing middle finger with closed hand, as this will be regarded as an insult. Some eye contact is expected but the gaze should not be held for too long.

South America

South America comprises a climate ranging from very hot in the north to cold in the south and in the mountain areas of the East coastal region. The large countries of Brazil and Argentina dominate, with the other countries mainly bordering the edge of the continent. In terms of trade, South America is made up of a small number of mainly moderately developed countries.

Greetings

In the north of the region, greetings are friendly and effusive with a light handshake lasting several seconds and with good eye contact. Women may cheek kiss on one or both cheeks, or may hold forearms. The verbal greeting will usually include title and family name.

In **Argentina**, greetings are a formal handshake and nod between both sexes. Verbal greetings include title and surname.

In **Chile**, when a woman enters a room men should rise and be prepared to shake her hand if she offers it. A seated woman need not rise and is not obliged to offer her hand. Verbal greetings include title and surname.

Dress

Business dress is conservative and smart, especially in **Argentina** and **Venezuela**, where appearance is important. Avoid wearing jeans unless they are well tailored and of smart appearance.

In **Brazil**, three-piece suits are an indication of executive status and two-piece suits an indication of office workers.

Proximity

As people in South America are generally very friendly, personal space is much smaller than in North America. Touching is to be expected and will be considered an insult if it is rebuffed.

Chileans and **Venezuelans** converse in close proximity, with good eye contact used to show interest and sincerity. In Venezuela, touching the other person's arm is common.

Colombians and **Ecuadorians** stand in close proximity when conversing but engage in less physical contact during conversation than other South Americans.

Gestures

South Americans may be quite expressive with their hand gestures whilst talking and good eye contact is expected. In some of the countries, the 'OK' gesture is a vulgar gesture and winking has a sexual connotation.

In **Brazil**, to indicate appreciation, pinch your earlobe between thumb and forefinger. To indicate good luck, make a fist with the thumb sticking out between the middle and index fingers. To indicate that you do not know the answer, flick your fingertips underneath your chin.

In **Argentina**, make good eye contact. Do not put your feet on furniture. Cover your mouth when you cough or yawn. Do not eat in the street or on public transport.

In **Chile**, cover your mouth if you yawn. Keep your hands above the table at all times during meals and never eat with your fingers. Do not pound your right fist into your left palm, as this is obscene. Holding your hand up with palm outwards and fingers spread means 'stupid'.

In **Colombia**, the 'OK' gesture, when placed as a circle in front of the nose indicates that someone is homosexual. Holding hands apart with two outward pointing fingers is obscene. It is impolite to yawn in public. Avoid putting your feet on furniture.

In **Costa Rica** and **Ecuador**, fidgeting with hands or feet is distracting and considered impolite.

In **Ecuador**, it is considered impolite to yawn or point at others in public.

Europe

Europe is divided mainly into the countries that make up the European Union and the former Soviet Union countries located in Europe. In terms of trade, Europe is made up of a large number of well-developed countries and some moderately developed countries.

Greetings

In the colder northern regions, greetings are confined to a short light-to-firm handshake between both sexes; brief eye contact and possibly a nod, especially in **Germany**, may be used. The verbal greeting will usually include title and family name. Also, a brief greeting such as, 'Good morning/afternoon/evening'. 'How do you do?' is acceptable, apart from in **The Netherlands** and **Ukraine**, where the only verbal exchange is your family name. Be aware that in **Hungary** the family name is listed before the other names. In **Russia**, do not shake hands with gloves on, as this is considered poor manners, and in **Germany**, shaking hands with the other hand in your pocket indicates a lack of respect.

In the warmer southern countries, greetings are more close and effusive and may include arm-clasping, hugging and cheek-kissing. In **Turkey**, a male should wait for a female to offer her hand, and some **Muslims** may avoid contact with the opposite sex altogether. Generally, throughout the region, verbal greetings include title and family name. Do not use first names until given permission to do so. You should be aware that the **French** sometimes introduce themselves by giving their family name before their first name – if in doubt, ask for clarification.

Dress

In the north, dress is usually conservative and formal or smart and casual. In the major cities, and especially in **France**, **Italy** and **Spain**, dress is often more expensive and fashionable. In **Russia**, women should dress conservatively and refrain from wearing trousers.

In the south, dress may be more relaxed and comfortable to suit the warmer climate, apart from **Portugal** and **Turkey**, where conservative, formal dress is worn throughout the year.

Proximity

In the colder north, people usually need a fairly large personal space and touching is generally to be avoided. In the warmer south, the opposite is usually true.

Gestures

People in the colder climates tend to be more reserved, are restrained in their use of gestures and speak more quietly than people in warmer climates. Speaking with hands in pockets or whilst chewing is impolite and pointing with the index finger may be considered rude. Sitting with an ankle resting on knee will be interpreted as being conceited. Some eye contact is expected but the gaze should not be held for too long, apart from in Ireland, were it is considered polite to do so. Winking is considered an inappropriate gesture in many of the countries.

The 'OK' gesture is a vulgar insult in **Belarus**, **Denmark** and **Norway**. In **Belgium** and **France**, the 'OK' gesture means zero or worthless.

In **Bulgaria**, the head nod signifies 'No'.

In **Romania**, making a fist with the thumb sticking out between the middle and index fingers is an insult but signifies 'Nothing' in **Belarus** and **Ukraine**.

In **Finland**, standing with arms folded is likely to be interpreted as arrogance. When sitting, do not cross your legs at the ankles or place an ankle on the knee. In **Finland** and **The Netherlands**, only take small portions of food, as it is rude to leave unconsumed food on the plate.

In the **Czech Republic**, higher-ranking and older people enter a room first and, where status is equal, men precede women. When eating, do not place your elbows on the table as this is poor etiquette.

In **Denmark**, women enter a room first and go down stairs before men but up stairs after men. Try not to turn your back on people, especially if having to squeeze past someone.

French people tend to be softly spoken and dislike loud voices. They have a great appreciation for the art of conversation and frequently interrupt each other, as polite argument is a form of entertainment to them.

Italians are very expressive with their hands when talking, so you should not place too much significance on this form of gesturing. Tapping the nose with the index finger signals a friendly warning to 'take care' because of danger or deceit. Flicking the chin with a finger signifies impatience but in **Portugal**, this gesture means the person does not have an answer.

Germans view business as being very serious and do not appreciate humour in a business context. In business meetings, age takes precedence over youth and older people are given precedence when entering and leaving the room. Chewing gum whilst holding a conversation is considered rude. Although Germans can consume large quantities of alcohol, public drunkenness is frowned upon.

Greeks may toss their head upwards to indicate 'No', which can be confused with a nod meaning 'Yes', so ensure you obtain a verbal agreement also. Be aware that Greeks may smile when they are angry. Greeks do not have a tradition of queuing, so do not show offence if you experience this.

Russians do not usually raise their voices, being generally reserved and sombre, and may be offended by loud and gregarious behaviour. If offered a drink by your Russian host, do not refuse, as this is a serious breach of etiquette. Try not to turn your back on people, especially if having to squeeze past someone.

In **Spain**, crossing your fingers is a friendly gesture and means 'good luck' or 'protection'. Pulling down on your eyelid means 'be alert' or 'I am alert'. Business negotiations are often long, arduous and chaotic, with much over-talking, and reverting to procedure and rules only as a last resort.

In **Sweden**, face a person who is talking to you, cross your arms as a sign of listening, and do not interrupt them. Swedes tend to be rather serious people and do not appreciate loud, extrovert behaviour.

In **Switzerland**, maintaining a good posture when standing or sitting is important and keep your hands out of your pockets. Do not chew gum in public and be aware that dropping litter is offensive and carries heavy fines.

In **Turkey**, 'No' is indicated by a backward tilt of the head with eyes half closed. Showing the soles of your feet is insulting. When facing another person, crossing your arms is rude. Women should not cross their legs.

In the **United Kingdom**, keep your gestures moderate and avoid gesturing with the index and middle fingers raised in a 'V' shape with palm facing you, as this is insulting. Tapping the nose with the index finger signals that something is to be kept secret. Personal space is important, so you should not stand or sit too close when conversing, and touching is generally inappropriate.

Asia

Asia is the most diverse of the continents in terms of races, religions, politics, cultures and languages. The region is made up of China, Japan, the Russian Federation, India, Pakistan, most of the Arab nations and a large number of smaller nations that make up the remainder of South East Asia.

Most Asians place a great deal of importance on relationships and building long-term relationships is essential for business success. The concept of 'saving face' is important and Asians will go to great lengths to save face and avoid embarrassment. Being made to 'lose face' is not easily forgotten or forgiven.

In terms of trade, Asia is made up of a mixture of well-developed, moderately developed and developing countries.

Greetings

The north contains the **Russian Federation**, whose people display little sign of affection in public and greetings are a short but firm handshake with exchange of title and family name only.

The **Arab nations** will generally use a light handshake when greeting non-Arabs. Their traditional greeting between males involves clasping the right hand and placing the left hand on the other's right shoulder whilst cheek kissing on both cheeks. Women accompanying Arab men may not be introduced, especially if they are wearing a veil. The greeting will usually be quite friendly and title and family name are given.

In **Israel**, women should wait for a man to offer his hand and should be aware that Orthodox Jewish males are unlikely to shake hands with women.

The **Chinese**, **Koreans** and **Japanese** traditionally bow or nod their head in a respectful manner, but when greeting people from other countries they will usually offer a light handshake and give title and family name. Be aware that, in **China**, **Korea** and **Vietnam**, the family name is listed before the other names.

In **China**, if you are welcomed with handclapping when visiting a gathering of people, the etiquette is to respond with handclapping also.

In **Indonesia**, greetings carry importance and formality and should not to be rushed. The traditional greeting is '*Selamat*', which means 'peace'. The verbal greeting may include title and family name. If given a business card, read it carefully, never write on it and do not put it in your back trouser pocket.

In **Japan**, if you are greeted with a bow, return with a bow as low as the one you received. The level to which you bow determines the status relationship between you and the other individual – a lower bow means a lower status. Bow from the waist with a straight back and keep your eyes lowered. Men should hold their palms flat against the sides of their thighs and women should hold their palms together pointing downwards in front of their thighs. There are many types and uses for bows in Japan, so if you will be doing business with the Japanese, make yourself familiar with bowing etiquette. The verbal greeting will usually include title and family name. Business cards are exchanged using both hands with a degree of reverence. The card should be examined carefully as a sign of respect and you should take special care in handling it. Do not write on the card or put it in you pocket or wallet, as these actions may be interpreted as defacing or disrespecting the card.

In **Malaysia**, **Singapore** and **Taiwan**, the handshake is gentle, sometimes involving both hands and may be prolonged for around ten seconds. The traditional **Malay** greeting is the *salaam*, which involves one or both hands gently touching but not clasping the other person's hands and then withdrawing to rest over their heart. The verbal greeting may include title and family name.

In **Taiwan**, you may be asked, 'Have you eaten?' as part of the greeting. This is a rhetorical question and the polite response is to affirm that you have eaten.

Most **Indians** will use the handshake but the traditional *namaste* of palms together beneath the chin as if praying in a reverent manner may be used. Generally, there is no public contact between men and women, so the *namaste* is a good alternative when greeting members of the opposite sex.

In **Thailand**, they use the *wai* greeting, which is similar to the *namaste* but with the palms held together in front of the face and the higher the hands are held the more respectful the greeting.

In **Pakistan**, the family name may be listed first or last. Often, the combination and order of the individual names that make up the complete name has a special meaning. Be aware that the use of a single name taken out of context of the full name may alter its meaning, so always ask how the person should be addressed.

Dress

In most of Asia, conservative, formal dress is worn throughout the year. In **Indonesia**, **Malaysia**, **Singapore** and many other countries in South East Asia, smart but less formal clothing may be worn to take account of the extreme heat and humidity.

In **Saudi Arabia** and many of the **Arab nations**, most of the body must be covered despite the heat. It is common to remove shoes before entering a building, so follow the lead of your host.

In **China**, women should avoid wearing revealing clothing, short-sleeved blouses and high-heeled shoes.

In **Japan**, the quality of your clothes will indicate your status, so 'dress to impress'. Wear shoes that are easy to take off and put on when visiting Japan, as you will do this often. Women should dress conservatively with minimum accessories, and should avoid wearing trousers and high-heeled shoes.

Proximity

Most **Russians**, **Chinese** and **Japanese** prefer a large personal space and do not like to be touched.

The other nations in the region are more expressive and overtly friendly, and close proximity and even touching may be acceptable as the relationship develops.

Gestures

Russians and **Chinese** gesture little and see no need for this form of flamboyance. In **China** and **Japan**, finger-pointing is considered rude, and the **Chinese** find placing fingers in the mouth revolting.

The **Japanese** do not like to say 'No' and will often say 'Yes' when they mean 'No'. To the Japanese, 'Yes' is an acknowledgement that they heard you. It is not an acknowledgement that they agree with you. If they indicate that 'it is difficult' or 'we need to consider it more carefully', they are probably saying 'No'. The Japanese read great significance into all forms of gesturing, so use gestures sparingly. The 'OK' gesture means 'money'. You should avoid pointing at people. Do no blow your nose in public. Keep eye contact brief. Facial expressions can have different meanings from those in other parts of the world and should be interpreted within the context of the other gestures. For example, a *smile* can mean either *joy* or *displeasure*, so use and interpret facial expressions with caution. The Japanese are quite comfortable with silence and use it to their advantage in many situations, especially when negotiating.

In **Hindu** and **Muslim** cultures, the custom is to use the right hand for food preparation and eating. The left hand is considered unclean due to its use in bodily hygiene and using it in social situations should be avoided as much as possible. Pointing the soles of your feet towards another person is offensive.

In **Saudi Arabia** and many of the **Arab nations**, gesturing is frequently used when speaking but pointing at another person is rude, as is an extended thumb with clenched hand gesture. It is not uncommon to see men walking hand-in-hand, as this is a sign of friendship. Conversations often go at a slow pace and you should not feel you have to speak during periods of silence. Do not forget that in Saudi Arabia, 'Yes' usually means 'possibly' and tipping the head back with a click of the tongue means 'No'.

In **India**, never touch another's head; finger pointing and beckoning is rude; never whistle, wink or point your feet at someone; always apologise if your foot touches another person; and leather accessories may cause offence, especially to **Hindus**.

In **Indonesia, Malaysia** and **Singapore**, bouncing the fist in the palm of the hand is an offensive gesture. Also, do not point with a finger or gesture with a closed hand and extended thumb. Never touch another person's head, especially children's heads.

The **Indonesians** are a softly spoken people, so do not raise your voice. It is not acceptable to express anger in public through tone of voice, loudness or body language. In conversation, if you hear 'Yes, but' it means '*No*'.

In **Taiwan**, do not touch another person's shoulders or head, especially with children. Do not touch or point with your feet, as feet are considered dirty. Also, do not discard food from your mouth back to your plate or bowl.

Africa

Africa is made up of countries with inhabitants of mainly Arab origin in the north, of mainly black African origin in the central to southern regions and of mainly mixed black and white origin in the extreme south. In terms of trade, Africa is made up of a large number of developing countries, some moderately developed countries and a few well-developed countries.

Greetings

The **Arab nations** will generally use a light handshake when greeting non-Arabs. Their traditional greeting between males involves clasping the right hand and placing the left hand on the other's right shoulder whilst cheek-kissing both cheeks. Women accompanying men may not be introduced. The greeting will usually be quite friendly and title and family name are given.

The many **Black African nations** have their own forms of greeting but a long gentle handshake and name will usually be offered to non-Africans.

In the developed areas of **South Africa** a short firm handshake with title and family name will be given.

Dress

In **Egypt** and the **Arab nations**, modest formal clothes covering most of the body should be worn and wearing jewellery, especially necklaces, should be avoided by men.

The **Black African nations** will wear either formal clothing or their traditional local dress. You are advised to wear conservative formal clothing suitable for the hot climate.

In **South Africa**, dress is fairly casual but for business you should wear conservative clothing suitable for the hot climate.

Proximity

People in the region are generally open, expressive and friendly, and close proximity and touching are usually acceptable as the relationship develops.

Gestures

In the **Hindu** and **Muslim** world, the custom is to use the right hand for food preparation and eating. The left hand is considered unclean due to its use in bodily hygiene and using it in social situations should be avoided as much as possible. Pointing the soles of your feet towards another person is offensive. In much of **South Africa**, the feet are also considered unclean and should not be used to touch or move things.

In **Egypt** and many of the **Arab nations**, gesturing is frequently used when speaking but pointing at another person is rude, as is the thumb up with clenched hand gesture.

In **Egypt**, when dining, leaving some food on your plate symbolises abundance and is considered a compliment to your host. Do not tap your two index fingers together as this is a crude gesture meaning 'Will you sleep with me?'.

Despite the political and tribal difficulties in many of the **Black African nations**, the people are usually hospitable, friendly, gentle and courteous. To be successful with them, demonstrate the same qualities to establish empathy and rapport.

In many of the **African nations**, as in the Muslim world, there is a preference for using the right hand, so use this hand to give and take things.

Australasia and Oceania

Australasia and Oceania comprises the countries of Australia, New Zealand, New Guinea and the Oceanic Islands of the southern Pacific Ocean. In terms of trade, the region is made up of the well-developed countries of Australia and New Zealand and developing countries such as New Guinea and the islands of Oceania.

Greetings

In **Australia** and **New Zealand**, a moderately firm, brief handshake with good eye contact, and giving title and family name is the norm. Women may shake hands or, in **Australia**, may give a cheek kiss. In the greeting, avoid the overuse of 'G'day': use 'Hello' or some other verbal greeting.

In **New Guinea** and the **Oceanic Islands**, people will have their own forms of greeting but they will usually offer a light courteous handshake to foreigners and give their name.

Dress

In **Australia** and **New Zealand**, business dress is conservative but clothing should take account of the seasonal climate.

In the other countries, dress conservatively and to suit the hot climate.

Proximity

Australians are generally open, friendly and direct but reserved in terms of the personal space they require, so do not stand or sit too close.

New Zealanders are often softly spoken and are more reserved than Australians, so use a moderate tone of voice and allow them ample personal space.

Gestures

In **Australia**, extended eye contact is the norm and indicates the person is trustworthy. Do not gesture with one or two fingers, as this is considered rude. Also, avoid winking and touching.

In **New Zealand**, keep your gestures moderate and avoid gesturing with the index and middle fingers raised in a 'V' shape, as this is considered rude.

INSTANT TIP

Do not lose business and make enemies: body language is just like a foreign language – the wrong gesture is as bad as the wrong word.

References

Comer, M. J., Ardis, P. M. and Price, D. (1992) *Bad Lies in Business: The Commonsense Guide to Detecting Deceit in Negotiations, Interviews and Investigations*, New York: McGraw Hill.

Fast, J. (1978) *Body Language*, New York: M Evans & Co Inc.

French, J. P. R. and Raven, B. (1960) 'The Basis of Social Power', in S. Cartwright and A. Zander (eds.), *Group Dynamics*, New York: Harper & Row, pp. 607–23.

Lambert, D. (1996) *Body Language* (Collins GEM), London: Harper Collins.

Morris, D. (1978) *Manwatching: Field Guide to Human Behaviour*, London: Triad Books.

Morrison, T. and Conaway, W. A. (2006) *Kiss, Bow or Shak Hands*, Massachusetts: Adams Media.

Thomas, D. C. and Inkson, K. (2003) *Cultural Intelligence*, San Francisco: Berrett-Koehler.

Index